MW00526864

BASIL OF CAESAREA

Cascade Companions

The Christian theological tradition provides an embarrassment of riches: from Scripture to modern scholarship, we are blessed with a vast and complex theological inheritance. And yet this feast of traditional riches is too frequently inaccessible to the general reader.

The Cascade Companions series addresses the challenge by publishing books that combine academic rigor with broad appeal and readability. They aim to introduce nonspecialist readers to that vital storehouse of authors, documents, themes, histories, arguments, and movements that comprise this heritage with brief yet compelling volumes.

TITLES IN THIS SERIES:

Reading Paul by Michael J. Gorman

Theology and Culture by D. Stephen Long

Creationism and the Conflict over Evolution by Tatha Wiley

Justpeace Ethics by Jarem T. Sawatsky

Reading Bonhoeffer by Geffrey B. Kelly

Christianity and Politics in America by C. C. Pecknold

The Letter to the Hebrews in Social Scientific Perspective by David A. deSilva

FORTHCOMING TITLES:

Philippians in Context by Joseph H. Hellerman

Basil of Caesarea

A Guide to His Life and Doctrine

Andrew Radde-Gallwitz

CASCADE *Books* • Eugene, Oregon

BASIL OF CAESAREA
A Guide to His Life and Doctrine

Cascade Companions 16

Cascade Books
An Imprint of Wipf and Stock Publishers
199 W. 8th Ave., Suite 3
Eugene, OR 97401

www.wipfandstock.com

ISBN 13: 978-1-60608-132-7

Cataloging-in-Publication data:

Radde-Gallwitz, Andrew

Basil of Caesarea : a guide to his life and doctrine / Andrew Radde-Gallwitz

Cascade Companions 16

xvi + 178 p. ; 20.5 cm. Includes bibliographical references and index.

ISBN 13: 978-1-60608-132-7

1. Basil, Saint, Bishop of Caesarea, ca. 329–379. I. Title. II. Series.

BR1720 B3 R15 2012

Manufactured in the U.S.A.

To Mark

Contents

Preface and Acknowledgments ix

Abbreviations xii

Timeline xiv

Introduction 1

1 Basil's "Conversion" 22

2 Eunomius: Basil's Opponent and His Context 43

3 The Theology of the Only-Begotten Son (*Against Eunomius* 1–2) 64

4 *Against Eunomius* 3 and the Beginning of Debate over the Spirit 78

5 Basil's Career: From *Against Eunomius* to *On the Holy Spirit* 90

6 *On the Holy Spirit* 108

7 Christ's Saving Economy: Basil Confronts Apollinarius 121

8 Basil's Final Years 133

Conclusion 141

Works by Basil 151

Primary Sources 161

Secondary Sources 167

Name and Subject Index 171

Scripture Index 176

Preface and Acknowledgments

Basil of Caesarea never wanted to change anything. Yet, he was a leading light in a generation of Christians who adapted to sweeping changes in the church and society, and in the process they shaped Christianity as we know it. Whenever we modern Christians recite the doxology—"Glory be to the Father, to the Son, and to the Holy Spirit . . ."—we are standing on the shoulders of giants like Basil, who helped Christians understand what such language has to teach us about God and ourselves. Whenever we struggle for social justice or for unity among Christians, we are tracking his footsteps, knowingly or unknowingly. Even those of us who occasionally despair over the state of the churches will find that we are often echoing Basil's own frustrations—though, of course, in the face of issues he could not have foreseen. This volume offers a guide through Basil's life and works. I have sought primarily to address readers who are interested in Christian theology and history but who have little background in it, while at the same time offering new perspectives that would be of interest to more seasoned scholars.

Despite his brilliance, Saint Basil was not isolated as an individual thinker, but was immersed in a network of friends and supporters. It is often remarked that today's scholarly life is a solitary one. I have had the good fortune of being alone together with some wonderful friends and colleagues, both inside and outside the academy. They continue to illumine and encourage my study of Basil and his times. I would like to thank Michel Barnes, who first suggested that I write this book—though I trust that readers will not hold the results of his request against him. Lewis Ayres continues to be an invaluable and generous conversation partner and a wise mentor. This book has benefited greatly from the work of many others; I especially want to thank Khaled Anatolios, John Behr, Volker Drecoll, Steve Hildebrand, Susan Holman, Philip Rousseau, Anna Silvas, and Raymond Van Dam—and to recommend their scholarship to the interested reader. I am grateful for the support of the Theology Department at Loyola University Chicago. A generous summer stipend in 2010 from Loyola's College of Arts and Sciences enabled me to draft a substantial portion of this book. I also thank Pat Reardon for truly helpful writing advice. Chris Spinks at Cascade Books has been patient and helpful throughout the entire process.

My deepest scholarly debt is to Mark DelCogliano. Not only did Mark share with me his translations of Basil's homilies in advance of publication, but he also carefully read my entire manuscript, sometimes in multiple drafts, and offered extensive comments that greatly improved the book. My regular conversations with Mark and our ongoing exchange of ideas have shaped these pages in more ways than I could acknowledge in the notes. In gratitude for his friendship and his wisdom, I dedicate this book to Mark.

I am once again in debt to Kristen Radde-Gallwitz. Her patient encouragement and insightful advice have seen me through many stages of this "little" project. I had read the following passage by Basil long before writing this book, but until our Samuel came along, I had not grasped its force—I quote it for Sam and Kristen with all my love: "Even if we did not know what God is from his goodness, yet, from the very fact that we are made by him, we ought to feel an extraordinary affection for him and cling to a constant remembrance of him, as infants do to their mothers."[1]

1. Basil, *LR* 2 (trans. Wagner, 236).

Abbreviations

AA	Eunomius, *Apology for the Apology*
Apol.	Eunomius, *Apology*
CH	*Church History*
D	Deferrari, Roy J., trans., *Basil: Letters*, 4 vols. (Loeb Classical Library 190, 215, 243, 270; Cambridge, MA: Harvard University Press, 1926–34)
ep./epp.	*epistle(s)*
ET	English translation
Eun.	*Against Eunomius*
FotC	The Fathers of the Church (Washington, DC: Catholic University of America Press, 1947–)
GNO	*Gregorii Nysseni Opera* (Works of Gregory of Nyssa; Leiden: Brill, 1960–)
G. Naz.	Gregory of Nazianzus
G. Nyssa	Gregory of Nyssa
Hex.	Basil, *Hexaemeron* (*Homilies on the Six Days of Creation*)
hom.	*homily*
LXX	Septuagint (Greek translation of the Hebrew Scriptures)
LR	Basil, *Longer Responses*

NPNF[2]	P. Schaff and H. Wace, eds., *A Select Library of the Nicene and Post-Nicene Fathers of the Christian Church*, Second Series, 14 vols. (Peabody, MA: Hendrickson, 1994 [1890–1900])
PG	J.-P. Migne, ed., Patrologia Cursus Completus: Series Graeca (Paris, 1857–86)
Ps./Pss.	Psalm(s)
or.	*oration*
SC	Sources Chrétiennes (Paris: Cerf, 1941–)
Spir.	Basil, *On the Holy Spirit*
SR	Basil, *Shorter Responses*

Timeline

325	Council of Nicaea
329/30	Basil is born
337	Emperor Constantine dies, is succeeded by his sons Constans and Constansius II
350	Constans dies; Constantius II is sole emperor
355	Basil abandons rhetorical studies in Athens, returns to Caesarea
357	Basil is baptized (probably after his ascetic tour), begins ascetic retreat
360	Council of Constantinople (under Constantius II)
361	Constantius II dies, Julian is made emperor and abandons Christianity
362	Basil is ordained presbyter in Caesarea
363–365	Basil's retires to Pontus for a second ascetic retreat
363	Emperor Julian is killed in battle against the Persians, is succeeded by Jovian
364	Emperor Jovian dies; Valentian succeeds him and makes Valens his co-emperor; Synod of Lampsacus

364/65	Basil writes *Against Eunomius*
365	Basil resumes pastoral duties in Caesarea
367	Synod of Tyana
369-70	Famine begins in Cappadocia
370	Basil is consecrated as bishop of Caesarea
372	Basil consecrates Gregory of Nyssa and Gregory of Nazianzus as bishops
375	Basil writes *On the Holy Spirit*
378	August: Valens dies in battle at Adrianople; late in the year: Basil dies
381	Council of Constantinople (under Theodosius)

Introduction

Valens was a military man who had been raised to the purple as Roman emperor by his brother, Valentinian. He was known to have a ferocious temper. And he was a Christian who was not above throwing his weight around in disputes among church leaders. According to one story, a group of eighty Christian clergymen grew tired of his abuse—for what exact reason they were oppressed, we do not know—and came to the city of Nicomedia to petition the emperor. Furious, Valens sent them all off on a ship, ostensibly into exile. When the vessel had sailed a ways into the gulf, under prior orders from the emperor it was set on fire by the crew and all eighty were burned to death, while the crew escaped.[1]

On January 6, 372, the feast of the Theophany, in the Cappadocian city of Caesarea, Valens showed up at the liturgy, which was presided over by the city's bishop, Basil. Basil, it happens, taught a different version of Christian doctrine than the one Valens favored. Basil's doctrine took its inspiration from the creed produced at the Council of Nicaea in 325, which is the basis of the confession of faith recited by millions of Christians today. Nicaea's creed proclaimed that the Son of God is "of the same substance"

1. Socrates, *CH* 4.16.

as God the Father and "from the substance of the Father." Valens had learned Christianity of a different kind, one suspicious of Nicaea's attempt to make the Son fully equal to God. Valens and his partisans objected to the Nicene Creed; the bishops he supported found it better to omit the language of "substance" altogether. Valens was in the midst of purging the eastern empire of any bishop opposed to him, and Basil was one of the few left standing. We are told that on one occasion, some time before Valens' visit to Caesarea, he had sent his prefect Modestus to coerce Basil. Modestus offered full imperial support to Basil on one condition: that he drop "of the same substance" from the creed.[2] "Impervious to threats and influence," Basil refused.[3] The implication was not lost on anyone: Basil was calling the emperor's religion a sham maintained by force rather than genuine faith.

Valens' personal entry into Caesarea in January 372, together with the vast imperial retinue, would obviously not have gone unnoticed. The stage was set for a dramatic showdown, and it is little wonder that the episode features prominently in the tales told of Basil by his admirers after his death. Valens' entourage entered Basil's church with him. It must have been an awesome and terrifying scene. But in the account of Basil's friend, Gregory of Nazianzus, it was Valens and not Basil who was shaken:

> Upon [Valens'] entrance he was struck by the thundering roll of the Psalms, by the sea of heads of the congregation, and by the angelic rather than human order which pervaded the sanctuary and its precincts: while Basil presided over his people, standing erect, as the Scripture says of Samuel (1 Samuel

2. G. Nyssa, *Eun.* 1.136.

3. G. Naz., *or.* 43.51 (*NPNF*[2] 7:411).

> 19:20), with body and eyes and mind undisturbed, as if nothing new had happened, but fixed upon God and the sanctuary, as if, so to say, he had been a statue, while his ministers stood around him in fear and reverence. At this sight, and it was indeed a sight unparalleled, overcome by human weakness, his eyes were affected with dimness and giddiness, his mind with dread.[4]

As Christian emperor, Valens was expected to present gifts during the eucharistic celebration. As he approached the altar, he was so stunned that he nearly tripped and fell.

Afterwards, Valens and Basil spoke. Their conversation is not recorded. According to Gregory, Basil's wise words so moved Valens that it marked "the beginning and first establishment of the Emperor's kindly feeling towards us; the impression produced by this reception put an end to the greater part of the persecution which assailed us like a river."[5] As Basil reported in a letter to Elias, the Governor of the province of Cappadocia, "the great Emperor . . . has allowed us to govern the churches ourselves."[6]

More than simply *allowing* Basil to govern the churches of Cappadocia, Valens actively supported him. He set him in charge, together with another bishop, of appointing new bishops for the Roman province of Armenia Minor and the client kingdom of Armenia, a crucial buffer with the Persian Empire. Roman emperors wished desperately to control affairs there and sought to use ties of Christian fellowship to spread their influence. Furthermore, Valens patronized Basil's massive charitable efforts in Caesarea,

4. Ibid., 43.52 (*NPNF*[2] 7:412).

5. Ibid. Theodoret, writing much later, describes an earlier conversation before the liturgy in his *CH* 4.16.

6. Basil, *ep.* 94.

which included new buildings dedicated to housing and feeding the poor, as well as hospitals and schools for vocational training.[7]

These acts of support and patronage demand explanation. Indeed, one must wonder why Basil was not sent into exile like so many of his allies. It is not that Valens was won over to Basil's cause or convinced of his doctrine. The emperor continued his assault on other, less fortunate supporters of the Nicene Creed. In 375, his agents had Basil's brother and many others sent into exile. Our sources seem to attribute Basil's success simply to his force of character. We must treat these sources, which are uniformly biased against Valens, with caution. But, even when read with appropriate suspicion, our sources seem to reveal that Valens saw Basil less as theologically persuasive and more as politically immobile.

As we embark upon a study of Basil's theology, it is important to register that he did not write in a position of detached, "academic" isolation. His words had real-world consequences. When he wrote, his typical purpose was not so much to persuade a neutral audience as to solidify connections he already had, or to establish new networks of friends and allies. This might seem distastefully "political" to modern readers. We are accustomed to the particularly modern split between politics, which is about pragmatic problem solving, and theology, which is often dismissed (I would say unjustly) as inconsequential, tedious wrangling about religious minutiae. That is how the powers that be in our cultural and symbolic world divide things up; it was not so in Basil's day. Theology then was written within a network of friends, potential friends, and enemies. The

7. See Theodoret, *CH* 4.16. It is likely that this patronage began before the meeting in 372.

network was always shifting: one bit of slander on your character and your friends could abandon you; with a careful campaign of letter writing, an enemy could come around; a stranger could become a brother simply by sending a response letter and acknowledging fellowship. In an empire that was slowly becoming Christian, theology had grave practical consequences.

St. Basil the Great lived from around 330 to 378. He cut a massive figure in his day. Although he is one of the most influential figures in Christian history, his work is typically read today only by professional scholars. This is of course understandable given the distance between his time and ours. But, for centuries, Basil's writings, or at least excerpts from them, were part of an informal curriculum of "must-reads" for educated Christians. They were translated into several languages. In Byzantine tradition, Basil was remembered as one of the Three Holy Hierarchs, together with his friend Gregory of Nazianzus and their younger contemporary John Chrysostom. Medieval Christianity was a traditional culture that looked to the past for inspiration. We often think of ourselves differently, as separated from the "premodern" world by a vast gulf. However, at the same time, many Christians today perceive a spiritual anemia in modern culture and in modern Christianity itself, and desire to explore their own tradition more deeply. Their goal is not to escape the modern world, but to thicken it; they want more interesting options than sentimentality or rationalism, fundamentalism or liberalism, traditionalism or progressivism, the nauseating rhetoric of right and left. To those who are so inclined, Basil is a worthy study. Yet, readers of Basil will not find a mythical Golden Age when all Christians were united and harmony reigned in the churches. Basil and his contemporaries have lessons for

Christians today, but they are not as obvious as this. What we see is that the struggle for community of life, of affection, and of belief was as difficult and as necessary then as it is now and that friendship and Christian kinship are beautiful but fleeting projects full of irony and risk.

Already in his day, Basil's name was known throughout the Christian world, among friend and foe—and those who weren't quite sure what to make of him. Most of his career was spent in the Roman provinces of Pontus and Cappadocia in Asia Minor (modern Turkey). From 370 until his death, he was bishop of the church in Caesarea (today, Kayseri), the capital city of Cappadocia. But his travels took him around the Eastern Mediterranean: to Constantinople and Athens for education as a rhetorician; to Syria, Mesopotamia, Palestine, and Egypt to learn the lifestyle of ascetic Christianity; to Armenia to supervise elections of bishops. Basil's accomplishments were manifold: he wrote instructions for monastic communities; he organized relief for victims of poverty and famine in Caesarea; he corresponded with major ecclesiastical and political figures as far apart as Alexandria and Rome; and, in letters, sermons, and theological treatises, he provided a snapshot of Christian doctrine in its formative period. It is to his works on doctrine that we give most of our attention in this book. The following chapters seek to acquaint the student with Basil's works on the Trinity, in particular on the divinity of Christ and of the Holy Spirit, and thereby to introduce the historical origins of these central Christian beliefs.

Compared with others of his time, we are unusually well supplied with sources of information on Basil's life. In his introduction to Basil, Anthony Meredith reminds us that, "With the exceptions of Cicero and St. Augustine, we probably know more about him than about any other ancient writer."[8] From Basil himself, we have quite a number of writings. This is no accident; when an author's work survives from antiquity, this typically means that people found it, for whatever reason, worth the labor of copying by hand. Basil's surviving work includes:

- Over three hundred letters, several of which will be discussed here.
- The three-book work *Against Eunomius*. This work is discussed at length in chapters 3 and 4 of the present book, with comments on its context in chapter 2.
- A treatise *On the Holy Spirit*. We will examine this in detail in chapter 6.
- An address *To Young Men On the Value of Greek Literature*.
- Forty-nine extant homilies. These include twenty-five numbered homilies on various topics, from the Trinity to fasting to social justice; a series of nine homilies on the creation story in Genesis, entitled *On the Six Days of Creation*; and fifteen homilies on the Psalms. Additionally, there are two homilies *On the Creation of Humanity*, which are sometimes attributed to Basil by scholars, though without any certainty.
- A corpus of ascetic writings. These include two collections of responses to questions on the ascetic life (*Shorter Responses* and *Longer Responses*), a compendium of topically arranged biblical verses entitled *Morals*, and two prefaces to the *Morals* meant to exhort the reader to ascetic discipline.
- A two-book work *On Baptism*.

8. Meredith, *Cappadocians*, 20.

- It is likely, though far from certain, that Basil played some role in constructing or editing the eucharistic liturgy that bears his name (the Anaphora of St. Basil).
- A number of works have been transmitted under Basil's name, but are either certainly or at least likely not authentic. These include several homilies, including one on Psalm 37, which is actually by Eusebius of Caesarea. Also in this category is a *Commentary on Isaiah*, a work of *Admonition to a Spiritual Son*, and several short ascetic sermons (some of which are misleadingly included in Sr. Monica Wagner's translation of Basil's ascetic works).[9]

Outside of Basil's corpus there are several valuable sources:

- Gregory of Nazianzus, *or.* 43. Basil's friend Gregory preached this in 382 or 383 in Caesarea. It is an encomium of Basil's virtues, but includes many details on his life.
- Gregory of Nazianzus, letters. Several of Gregory's letters are either addressed to Basil or inform us about events in Basil's life.
- Gregory of Nyssa, *Encomium on His Brother Basil.* Gregory delivered this speech in praise of his brother on January 1 of 380 or 381, which became the feast day for St. Basil.
- Gregory of Nyssa, *Life of Holy Macrina.* Gregory wrote this after his and Basil's sister Macrina passed away in 379. It includes a great deal of information on the family, including a story of Basil's "conversion" to the ascetic and ecclesiastical life.

9. The first three works in Wagner's collection are considered spurious, as well as the homily *On Mercy and Justice.*

- Gregory of Nyssa, *Against Eunomius*. After Basil's death, Gregory took up the struggle against Eunomius. In this three-book work, he defends Basil's doctrine and character, providing valuable information.
- The fifth-century church historians discuss Basil's career and events in the church and empire at this time. These are Rufinus, Socrates, Sozomen, and Theodoret (all on the pro-Nicene side and therefore sympathetic to Basil) and Philostorgius (on the Eunomian side and therefore hostile). Basil is also mentioned in Jerome's work *On Famous Men*, from the early 390s.
- For the Roman Empire during Basil's life, we have an important witness in the historian Ammianus Marcellinus. For firsthand accounts of the intellectual, social, and political life of the eastern half of the empire, we have orations by Themistius and surviving orations and letters by the famous pagan rhetorician Libanius, with whom Basil studied briefly. Additionally, there are accounts in Eunapius' *Lives of the Sophists* about Basil's teachers Himerius and Prohaeresius in Athens.
- Two late hagiographies have survived. An *Encomium on Basil the Great* survives, which is falsely attributed to Ephrem the Syrian. Another work, the *Life and Miracles of Basil*, was traditionally attributed, falsely, to Basil's friend and protégé Amphilochius of Iconium. It was likely written in the sixth or seventh century. Since its contents are largely legendary and anachronistic, it is of little value for the study of Basil's life, though it was widely read in the early Middle Ages.[10]

10. For this text, see Corona, *Aelfric's Life*. Aelfric's Anglo-Saxon text of the life, itself based on a Latin translation from a Greek original, is translated into English by Corona on pp. 153–89. Her intro-

In one sense, the sheer bulk of evidence makes our task easy. In contrast with other ancient figures (Jesus, for instance), there are fewer gaping holes in our knowledge of Basil's adult life. In another sense, however, the burden shifts from simply reconstructing historical events (about which we can often come to consensus), to interpreting the theological meaning of documents, which is often a difficult and contentious business. Was Basil the leading defender at his time of the doctrine of the Trinity, and especially of the divinity of the Holy Spirit? Or did he attempt an ill-advised compromise with those who rejected the notion that the Spirit deserves equal glory with God and Christ? Was he merely a church administrator who lacked the intellectual rigor and spiritual depth required to tackle such issues well? Or was he a profound thinker in his own right? One cannot consistently answer in the affirmative to all of these, but one can find reputable scholars supporting each interpretation. How we answer these questions—and others like them—will determine not only how we understand Basil as an individual, but also how we think about Christian doctrine as we have inherited it. Is it an incoherent mix of irreconcilable ideas or the product of a profound theological vision? Are the church's creeds mere political documents meant to exclude deviants and to enforce strict codes of belief? Can they continue to illuminate prayer and spirituality today? My hope is that, after reading this book, the reader will be better able to address questions like these. Most importantly, I hope this book invites the reader to answer them by studying primary sources such as those listed above. In particular, we will foreground Basil's two major doctrinal works, *Against Eunomius* and

duction contains material of interest for the reception of Basil's image and of his works in the West.

On the Holy Spirit, though, as we will see, to understand each work we must place it into its historical context and see how its themes appear in other works by Basil, from letters to sermons. The book is meant as an invitation to read Basil's own words and thereby to enter into conversation with readers since his own day who have tried to figure him out. The works have a clarity and consistency of vision and an undeniable rhetorical power. Still, they can be difficult. It is for this reason that the exposition in the chapters that follow often includes quotations from the works themselves, some of them lengthy and followed by explanation. Ancient writing is very different from modern writing, and some guidance might be necessary for those approaching it for the first time.

Given the variety and the quantity of the surviving evidence, any single book on Basil must be selective. I make no pretensions to cover every aspect of Basil's career. Fortunately, there is already an excellent biographical study of the various aspects of Basil's life and career in their broader historical context by Philip Rousseau.[11] There are outstanding studies of Basil as a church leader,[12] as a master of Christian spirituality,[13] and as a legislator of monastic communities.[14] Basil's relation to the Greek philosophical traditions has recently been reconsidered.[15] There is a helpful overview of the theology of the three so-called Cappadocian Fathers—Basil, Gregory of Nazianzus, and Gregory of Nyssa.[16] There are important scholarly studies

11. Rousseau, *Basil of Caesarea.*

12. Fedwick, *Church and Charisma*; Sterk, *Renouncing the World.*

13. Holmes, *Life Pleasing.*

14. Silvas, *Asketikon.*

15. Ayres and Radde-Gallwitz, "Basil of Caesarea."

16. Meredith, *Cappadocians.* The label "Cappadocian Fathers"

of Basil's Trinitarian thought in English,[17] French,[18] and German.[19] There are reference works devoted to Basil.[20] Unlike most of these, the current book does not have professional scholars as its primary audience. This study also differs in that it seeks to integrate the many aspects of Basil's career (Rousseau's study being the exception here), and in the interpretation it offers of his Trinitarian writings. I suggest that we must avoid two problematic approaches to Basil's works on the Trinity. First, we should not view Basil's thought as developing from one doctrinal party to another—from Homoiousian to Nicene (labels that will be explained as we go). We will see that the lines between these "parties" were erasing in Basil's lifetime. Where there is "development," it can be explained in better terms than as "switching parties." Moreover, there are great continuities across Basil's writings that are masked by an overemphasis on development. Second, it is not our task to judge whether Basil was orthodox or heretical. When modern writers make such judgments, they typically tell us more about the writer's preferences than about the historical figures being studied. While nothing presented in the following pages rules out the traditional image of Basil as an orthodox saint, it is neither the book's intention to defend Basil's orthodoxy nor to impugn it. While I will

---

for these three does not go back to their time, but is a construction of nineteenth-century German scholarship. Many theologians have lumped them together as if they taught a single theology, which is a problematic assumption.

17. Hildebrand, *Trinitarian Theology*.

18. Sesboüé, *Saint Basile*.

19. Drecoll, *Entwicklung*.

20. Fedwick, *Basil of Caesarea*. Volume 1 includes a list of Basil's works and a full chronological ordering of them, compiled by Fedwick. Fedwick also edited the five-volume *Bibliotheca*.

briefly discuss the growth of Basil's image as a teacher of the church in the book's conclusion, I am seeking merely an accurate summary of what he taught, why it mattered, how he reasoned, and what his aims were. If I suggest that he has much to teach any theologian, it is not because I am advocating his doctrine and condemning his opponents.

Although I will speak of "Basil's" Trinitarian theology, it is important to reiterate that Basil was not simply an individual thinker whose thought can be studied apart from his context. Basil was not merely advancing idiosyncratic theories, as a modern theologian might, with a narrow, academic audience as his or her target. Basil was talking about the public, shared language of the church—the grammar of its prayer, liturgy, and faith. Basil was helping to define Christian doctrine.

This term "doctrine" requires some comment. Among many modern intellectuals and laypersons, the idea of religious doctrine has fallen further out of fashion than that of the divine right of kings. Early Christian doctrine, such as that expressed in the Nicene Creed, can seem at its heart to be about the exercise of power, in particular about the coercive silencing of those who dissent. It can appear as simply a relic of a bygone era. Many modern theologians believe that those early Christians who were involved in writing and arguing about such creeds were committing something of a mistake, even in their original context. Christianity, on this interpretation, was never meant to be dogmatic. Its humanistic, religious, and ethical core was buried under layers of metaphysical speculation. Moreover, the political intrigue and violence that accompanied the development of creedal Christianity raise questions about its legitimacy. So goes the critique offered by such diverse thinkers as Thomas Jefferson and Adolf von Harnack, the great German Protestant church historian.

So why bother with a book on the doctrine of the Trinity in the fourth century? It is not enough to say that this doctrine is still binding on Christians today. While this is officially true for Catholic, Eastern Orthodox, and most Protestant Christians, actual attitudes among the faithful—clergy and laity alike—often more closely resemble the perspectives of Jefferson or Harnack than those of Basil. This book does not seek to "defend" traditional doctrine against modern criticism. It certainly offers no encouragement for *dogmatism* in the sense of absolutizing one's own limited perspective and refusing to value what is good and true in diverse cultures, religions, and philosophies. Nor, it goes without saying, would I like to see coercive force being used for religious aims. This book does aim to uncover more precisely *what doctrine was* in the early church. What did they think they were arguing about? If we can answer this, we might understand why Basil and others spent such tremendous energy over questions that can, at first glance, seem archaic to us. It is my belief that many of those who have criticized early Christian doctrine have misconstrued its nature. So what was doctrine?

We can begin the process of answering this by citing Basil's own words. In a letter he wrote in 372 to Valerian of Aquileia, a city along the northern Adriatic in Italy, Basil summarizes why agreement among Christians in doctrine matters. Basil had never met Valerian and had never traveled as far west as Aquileia. Basil is responding to a letter from Valerian that reports, to Basil's delight, that they share the faith of Nicaea. Basil notes that there are ongoing disagreements in his own regions. He expresses his hope as follows: "may the good teaching of our fathers who met at

Nicaea shine forth again, so that the doxology which is in harmony with saving baptism may be duly offered to the Blessed Trinity."[21]

A couple of points stand out. First, Basil refers to the bishops who met at the Council of Nicaea as "our fathers," that is, ancestors of Christians in Asia Minor and in Italy. Basil's and Valerian's common assent to Nicaea makes them, in a sense, brothers. Doctrine is meant to be a shared language for Christians that transcends local boundaries and guarantees ties of Christian kinship. In the modern world, we have divisions among the churches. At least until recently, we have not thought as often of the difficulty posed within a single communion by geographical differences and by the clash that inevitably happens when various local customs come into contact with each other. Today, the Anglican Communion is perhaps most visibly grappling with these issues, but the same problems confront the Roman Catholic Church and others. But often today we have a more "centralized" notion of church authority, as well as established procedures for meeting together and airing grievances. The church of Basil's day was not nearly as centralized. It can be thought of as a federation or network of local churches, each one led by a bishop and centered in one of the cities of the Roman Empire (and, in fewer cases, beyond its boundaries). The indigenous term for the network was "communion." Communion was predicated upon shared faith. Bishops had to recognize one another as broadly within this communion. Exchanges of letters can be visibly marked with anxiety as bishops seek recognition from one another. In his exchange with Valerian over matters of doctrine, Basil is not so much calling for an arcane debate as he is cementing an alliance. The task could be

21. Basil, *ep.* 91 (D 2:131, altered).

tricky indeed. We can easily imagine how hard it would be when two bishops fundamentally disagree, for instance, over *which* creed to endorse. But it is perhaps more difficult when two bishops claim the same creed, but interpret its decrees differently. As we will see, Basil faced both kinds of problems in his search for communion. But we should always bear in mind the search for communion as we study works of doctrinal debate; the authors of these works were testing the limits of the Christian family.

Second, when Basil speaks of the "doxology" which is "in harmony with saving baptism," he is referring to public worship, in particular forms of prayer that glorify God. His hope is that these will cohere with the tradition of baptism, as taught by Christ in Matthew 28:19, "in the name of the Father, the Son, and the Holy Spirit"—a verse he never tires of citing. To glorify God properly, one must do so in the same name invoked on Christians at their baptism. And one must understand this rightly: not in a strictly unitarian fashion as three titles for what is actually single—the error of the third-century Christian teacher Sabellius which is thereafter known as Sabellianism; nor as three separable beings only loosely connected; nor in any other order (Father, Spirit, Son, for instance). Basil's letter reveals the belief that only if one is "right" about doctrine can one reverence God rightly.[22] It was crucial to

22. See also Basil, *ep.* 159: ". . . as we are baptized, so also do we believe; as we believe, so also do we recite the doxology. Since then, baptism has been given to us by our Saviour in the name of the Father and of the Son and of the Holy Spirit, we offer the confession of our faith in accordance with our baptism, and in accordance with our faith we also recite the doxology, glorifying the Holy Spirit along with the Father and the Son, because we are convinced that He is not foreign to the divine nature" (D 2:395–97). Very similar language appears in *epp.* 125 and 210.

grasp the link between doctrine and worship, and to see how important it was to get worship right. Think back to Gregory of Nazianzus's depiction of Valens' entry into Basil's church. To be sure, we must take this with a grain of salt, recalling that it is written in a speech meant to glorify Basil. Yet, it is noteworthy that Gregory's perhaps idealistic vision portrayed Basil the bishop, presiding over the mysteries of Christian worship and arrayed in splendor with his fellow ministers, as a sight terrifying enough to scare the bejeezus out of the Roman emperor. This self-confident image of Christian worship conveys something of the awesome power believed to be in Basil's hands when he, as bishop, celebrated the Eucharist.

This emphasis on the practice of worship can appear foreign to modern, Western sensibilities. Since the Protestant Reformation of the sixteenth century, "belief" has been viewed as the central category of religion. Belief has been seen as only arbitrarily related to worship. A lot of people today agonize over whether or not to believe. But many, even among believers, view it as insignificant whether they express their beliefs ritually in worship. Hence the common self-description as "spiritual, but not religious." It is rare to find people expending energy on debates over various versions of ritual worship. Right or wrong, these assumptions can blind us to the Christianity of Basil's day, when a slight change in the form of the doxology used in public worship could lead to controversy. It is easy to dismiss this wrangling as tedious. But we must remember that ancient people as a rule—not just Christians, but also Jews and pagans—believed that religious ritual mattered. Though they differed greatly in their beliefs about the divine and in their religious practices, it was commonly (though not universally) held that to honor God or the gods appropriately is a basic human duty—in Basil's words, that the doxology must be "duly offered." In a reverse of our modern presuppositions, many ancient people viewed right belief as less important than cultic practice. This wasn't quite true for Basil. For him, belief and worship were so inextricably bound together that neither took precedence over the other. But this meant that questions of belief were threatening: if you do not know *whom* you are worshipping, how can you be sure that you are doing so rightly? When Basil's protégé and ally Amphilochius of Iconium was attacked by other Christians who disagreed with his doctrine, they asked him, "Do you worship what you know or what you do not know?"[23] These taunts reflect a real anxiety among Christians who were demonstrably divided in doctrine. If so, how did they know it was God they were worshiping? It was—and is—all too easy to fall into idolatry. In religious terms, this would violate the command to worship God alone; in sociological terms, it would erase the carefully constructed rhetorical lines Christians used to distinguish themselves from their pagan neighbors. Christians were supposed to be those who worship God "in spirit and truth" (John 4:24). It would have been no small embarrassment if Christians could not articulate this "truth" at all.

Basil's concerns about communion and worship should not be read as narrowly "spiritual" concerns, isolated in a separate sphere marked "religion." By his day, as we have already seen, they had become concerns of state in the Roman Empire. Part of why the debates of his time were so loud was that Christian leaders were hoping to catch the ear of the emperor himself—and hoping they weren't asked how they'd like a boat ride. The public character of religion in the ancient world needs to be borne in

23. See Basil, *ep.* 234.

mind. The emperor had traditionally been—and continued to be throughout Basil's lifetime—chief priest (*pontifex maximus*). Indeed, emperors themselves had been revered as gods. Even with the transition to Christianity, emperors continued to play a role in ensuring divine favor and protection for the empire and her citizens.[24]

So then, we have three factors that help to explain the intensity of the doctrinal controversies of Basil's day: the desire to establish communion among the churches, the connection between doctrine and worship, and the public consequences of religious practice. To these, I would add a fourth that will be of great importance in what follows: by the early Christian period, educated culture had come to be centered more and more on the interpretation of *texts.* This, again, is foreign to us. We value originality and creativity. To be sure, we might read old books. But our emphasis is on searching for new truths and, in a phrase one often hears around universities, creating new knowledge. In the late ancient world, the real truth is not made; it is there to be discovered in the classic books. In the Greco-Roman world of late antiquity, everyone learned to read Homer. Philosophers practiced their art by commenting on Plato or Aristotle. Rhetoricians learned to imitate classic orators. There was originality. But newness was shaped by tradition, and in particular by written classics.

There was a particularly Christian version of this, which was set forth most clearly by Origen in the third century and which fundamentally shaped subsequent theology. Christians looked to the Scriptures as their own classics, though they did not necessarily disdain the "pagan"

24. For a concise discussion of Constantine in light of the Roman tradition of imperial involvement in religion, see Drake, "Impact of Constantine."

traditions of Greece and Rome. Early Christian literature is shot through with citations of Scripture, allusions to biblical themes and characters, and creative adaptations of biblical imagery. Their goal was not to think originally, but to let the language of Scripture speak in new ways through them. Scriptural quotations, allusions, and themes appear in early Christian works for different reasons. They can convey divine commandments. They can provide aesthetic charm to a discussion of a difficult topic, like seasoning which makes a dish more palatable.[25] Other times, early Christians invoked Scripture because they were arguing against other Christians who had cited the same verse but understood it differently. This called for clarification and interpretation. We will see this repeatedly. Despite their disagreements, Christians of Basil's day agreed that the Scriptures contained the revelation of God. The various sides in the Trinitarian controversies emphasized their pet verses, but all parties had to offer a coherent account of all the relevant verses. They believed that the Scriptures speak consistently, even as they acknowledged that each biblical author is unique and many passages are almost impenetrably obscure. Basil, who defended the full divinity of the Son—as proclaimed, he believed, in verses like John 1:1, "In the beginning was the Word. The Word was with God and the Word was God"—had to discuss verses like John 14:28, where Jesus says, "The Father is greater than I." How can both verses be true? In analyzing Basil's major doctrinal works, we will emphasize that his thinking was grounded in biblical interpretation (also known as exegesis). For Basil, the biblical authors provide us with

25. For this metaphor, see the letter by Peter of Sebasteia to Gregory of Nyssa (both of them younger brothers of Basil): G. Nyssa, *ep*. 30. 5.

the exemplary thoughts on matters of Christian doctrine and Christian practice; it is our task to purify ourselves, intellectually and morally, so that we can grasp these and imitate them in our own thinking and acting. With these points of orientation in mind, let us turn to the story of how Basil came to be involved in the complicated disputes over doctrine in the fourth-century churches.

ONE

Basil's "Conversion"

Basil was born in AD 329 or 330, at a time when Christianity had become legally recognized in the Roman Empire and was emerging as a major force in public life. He would never share the experience of his paternal grandparents, who had been forced into hiding in the mountains of Pontus during the ferocious persecution of Christians by the Emperor Maximinus Daia in 311–12.[1] It was from this grandmother, Macrina the Elder, as well as his mother Emmelia, that Basil claimed to have first received his "conception of God."[2] Basil came from a family of eminent Christian virtue. He was the second oldest of ten children, nine of whom survived infancy. The names of five of these have come down to us as saints: Macrina (whose ascetic virtue was immortalized by her younger brother Gregory

1. See G. Nyssa, *Life of Macrina* (Callahan, 164); G. Naz., *or.* 43.5–8.

2. Basil, *ep.* 223.2 (D 3:299); *ep.* 204 (D 3:169).

in the *Life of Macrina*), Basil, Naucratius (an ascetic who cared for the elderly at his monastic retreat along the Iris River, but whose life was tragically cut short in a hunting accident), Gregory (known as Gregory of Nyssa), and Peter (who became bishop of Sebasteia around 381). The others' names are unknown, though we know they were daughters.[3]

When we speak of Basil "converting" as a young adult, we clearly do not mean that he adopted a different religion from that of his parents. Rather, we are describing the reorientation of values entailed by Christian commitment. In his early years, Basil was groomed to become an outstanding rhetorician, following his father, Basil the Elder, who was a professor of rhetoric—a "teacher of virtue"—in the city of Neocaesarea near the family's estate in Pontus.[4] It was a path bound to lead Basil to eminence and honor in society, either as a distinguished professor like his father or through service in local government or even the imperial administration. Basil was first educated in Neocaesarea under his father, with a combination of the classical curriculum and Christian piety. After Basil the Elder's death around 345, Basil proceeded to the schools of Caesarea, the Cappadocian metropolis where he would later serve as bishop. From there he went to the finest rhetorical schools the eastern Mediterranean had to offer, studying under the famous pagan orator Libanius, among others, in Constantinople for about a year and thence moving in 349 to Athens, still a center of Greek culture.

3. Gregory of Nyssa says there were four sons. It is quite possible, but not certain, that one of the daughters was the Theosebeia mentioned by Gregory of Nazianzus. For discussion, see Silvas, *Gregory of Nyssa*, 98–100.

4. G. Naz., *or.* 43.12.

Here he was reacquainted with his friend Gregory (who would later become known as Gregory of Nazianzus). Like Basil, Gregory was born in or around 330 to a wealthy, landowning family. Gregory's family owned an estate near Arianzum in Cappadocia.[5] His father, Gregory the Elder, came from a family devoted to the rather shadowy "Hypsistarian" cult of God Most High (*Hupsistos*), which was perhaps an amalgam of Jewish monotheism and rituals from Persia and elsewhere. Gregory the Elder converted to Christianity and became bishop of Nazianzus. Gregory (the younger)'s mother Nonna came from a Christian family. Basil and his friend Gregory had met early in life, probably in Caesarea in Cappadocia. Between that meeting and their reacquaintance in Athens, Gregory studied in Caesarea Maritima in Palestine and in Alexandria. Reunited in Athens, he and Basil pursued an advanced rhetorical education, which included reading philosophy, under the pagan Himerius and the Christian Prohaeresius.

Yet, Basil found Athens an "empty happiness" and, despite the efforts of his friend Gregory to persuade him to stay, Basil returned to Caesarea in 355.[6] According to his brother Gregory, he came home "excessively puffed up by his rhetorical abilities," thinking himself "better than the leading men in the district."[7] He took up a teaching post in Caesarea. One of his pupils was his younger brother Gregory, who would go on to be one of the finest Christian writers and thinkers of his generation. But Basil still hadn't withdrawn far enough from the pressures and complications of his career path, which, despite his father's example, Basil found to fit poorly with being Christian. In

5. For the location, see McGuckin, *Saint Gregory*, 2 n. 3.

6. G. Naz. *or.* 43.18.

7. G. Nyssa, *Life of Macrina* (Callahan, 167).

professional urban living Basil found the seeds of "countless evils."[8]

Basil was drawn to what he called the "philosophical life." This is "philosophy" in a different sense than is customary today. For Basil, it did not name an academic discipline or department, as in the modern university. For Christians of Basil's day, the term denoted a disciplined way of life in accordance with the gospel that involved some degree of renunciation of sex, family, homeland, and social status in order to cultivate wholehearted devotion to Christ. Philosophy meant a lifelong search for God, a continual, ongoing struggle and "training" (*askēsis* in Greek, whence "asceticism"). Among the Greeks and Romans, philosophy had long been understood as an entire way of life rather than simply something one studied. Christians made this term their own, using it to describe those who responded to Christ's call to take up the cross and follow him. With Christ's coming, the time for the command to "be fruitful and multiply" had passed; now, in Paul's words, "the time is short" and must be spent in disciplined watchfulness.[9]

News had travelled to Basil of famous Christian ascetics around the eastern Mediterranean, and he embarked upon a pilgrimage to see these living icons in Syria, Palestine, Mesopotamia, and Egypt.[10] In a later letter, Basil claims he was following the itinerary of Eustathius, an

8. Basil, *ep.* 2.

9. See Basil, *ep.* 160.

10. G. Naz. speaks of "voyages" (*ekdēmiai*) during Basil's time in Caesarea (*or.* 43.25). These are probably the journeys discussed in Basil's *epp.* 1 and 223. Basil speaks of his youthful enthusiasm for ascetics as living icons in *ep.* 223 (there speaking of ascetics in his home region of Pontus): ". . . I believed I had found an aid to my own salvation, and I considered the things that were seen as indications of things that were invisible" (D 3:295).

ascetic Christian born sometime before 300 who became bishop of Sebasteia in the Roman province of Armenia Minor and who was highly influential on the development of asceticism in the region.[11] Probably in 340 or 341, a small synod at Gangra in Paphlagonia (north-central Asia Minor) had condemned some of the excesses of Eustathius's ascetic teaching. He was accused of emphasizing celibacy so strongly that he condemned the married life for Christians. He preached Christian equality so emphatically that he undermined the subordination of women to men and of slaves to masters by urging them to change their style of hair and dress, markers that—then as now—were intimately bound up with status. We cannot be certain whether Eustathius actually taught these things, some of which admittedly sound more favorable to twenty-first-century Christian ears than to fourth-century ones. However, there was clearly something revolutionary in his understanding of the gospel. It appears that he also wanted to purify church leadership. Eustathius thought bishops themselves should not simply be administrators of church property, but spiritual persons, ascetics in fact. He established communities of ascetic Christians in or near urban areas, where they could perform acts of charity.[12] Eustathius became something of a mentor to Basil.[13]

In the meantime, however, Basil never caught up with Eustathius during his tour. It is hard to say exactly what Basil learned on his trip. Clearly, he returned with a

11. Basil, *ep.* 1. It is likely, but not certain, that the addressee of this letter—Eustathius the philosopher—is to be identified with Eustathius, bishop of Sebasteia.

12. See Elm, *Virgins of God*, 106–12.

13. See, e.g., Basil, *ep.* 244, where Basil speaks of his earlier service to Eustathius.

zeal for the ascetic life, though that zeal was the impetus for the journey in the first place. Perhaps he learned the custom of chanting the Psalms antiphonally. We know that later he introduced it in Pontus and Cappadocia. When certain Christians attacked this liturgical innovation, Basil justified the practice by saying it is universal among "the Egyptians . . . Libyans, the Thebans, Palestinians, Arabians, Phoenicians, Syrians, and those who dwell along the Euphrates," a list with some degree of correspondence to Basil's itinerary.[14] It has been suggested that Basil brought from Egypt the core of the eucharistic liturgy that bears his name. This is highly speculative. Basil was either newly baptized—a "neophyte"—or not yet baptized. In the latter case, he would most likely not have had access to the eucharistic prayer in Egypt during his time there. (In contrast, he could have attended prayer services that employed the antiphonal chant). If he was a neophyte, he was not yet ordained, so it is strange to attribute the writing of eucharistic prayers to him at this stage. Still, it is true that the eucharistic prayer he helped to craft bears resemblance to other prayers from Egypt. It makes most sense, however, to place his work on this anaphora (eucharistic prayer) later in his career, after becoming bishop.

It was most likely around the time of his return to Caesarea in 357 that Basil was baptized under the bishop Dianius. Baptism marked a revolution in his life. The rest of our book will in a sense be simply following Basil as he worked out the ramifications of this rebirth for his understanding of God. For now, we must note that Basil believed that baptism required that he emulate those icons of ascetic life he found around the eastern Mediterranean by renouncing his career ambitions. He gave up his father's

14. Basil, *ep*. 207 (D 3:189).

path. Baptism also brought Basil, perhaps reluctantly, into the orbit of the public ministry of the church. The pull was ultimately irresistible. Initially, however, Basil was not seeking any post in the church. He was after solitude. Basil left his post in Caesarea and returned home to the family estate near the town of Annisa in Pontus. In a secluded spot across the Iris River, Basil set up shop.

His sister, Macrina, had already professed the philosophical life in the 340s and had converted the villa into a kind of domestic monastic community. She even persuaded her mother to free the family's domestic servants.[15] In the *Life of Macrina*, Gregory of Nyssa attributes Basil's conversion to Macrina's influence. But Basil never says a word of this. In a letter from almost twenty years later, he likens his decision to abandon his hollow career path to waking up from a deep slumber.[16] He does not tell us *who* awoke him. In this later letter, he attributes his change of orientation to his reading of the gospel, which called him to sell all he had and give it to the poor. But, he continues, he needed flesh-and-blood examples to emulate. He found them not only in his pilgrimage, but even in his home region, in Eustathius and his associates.

We learn Basil's perspective on his ascetic retreat along the Iris River at the time he was making it from two letters inviting his friend Gregory to join him. In the first (*ep.* 14), he offers an idyllic description (*ekphrasis*) of the physical setting; surrounded by forest and river, it conspicuously

15. Her brother Gregory would go on to argue in his theological writings that slavery is inherently immoral: G. Nyssa, *Hom. 4 Eccl.* For more on the family's slaves, see Basil's *ep.* 37, with the interesting—and perhaps contradictory—note that the slaves were placed by Basil's parents in the trust of Basil's beloved, but unnamed, foster-brother, the son of Basil's nurse.

16. Basil, *ep.* 223.2 (D 3:293). This letter was written in 375.

contrasts with the urban life Basil and Gregory would have known together in Athens. In the second (*ep.* 2), he gets to the heart of the matter. The document became a classic in Eastern monastic tradition. He says he has been unable to find the tranquility he was seeking; he has carried his troubles with him, despite his change in locale and lifestyle. Still, he does outline what *ought* to happen: "We must try to keep the mind in tranquility."[17] Our lives bring with them a multitude of cares—the desire for children, concerns with the management of one's household (including watching over one's wife and protecting the rights of one's servants), business concerns, and so forth.

> There is but one escape from all this—separation from the world altogether. But withdrawal from the world does not mean bodily removal from it, but the severance of the soul from sympathy with the body, and the giving up [of] city, home, personal possessions, love of friends, property, means of subsistence, business, social relations, and knowledge derived from human teaching; and it also means the readiness to receive in one's heart the impressions engendered there by divine instruction. And making the heart ready for this means the unlearning of the teachings which already possess it, derived from evil habits. For it is no more possible to write in wax without first smoothing away the letters previously written thereon, than it is to supply the soul with divine teachings without first removing its preconceptions derived from habit.[18]

17. Basil, *ep.* 2 (D 1:9). The Greek for "in tranquillity" is *en hēsuchia(i)*. "Hesychasts," a word formed from this, would become a technical term in Greek Christian tradition for those who seek to live a life free of the disturbance of the passions and worldly thoughts.

18. Basil, *ep.* 2 (D 1:11).

Physical renunciation is necessary, but clearly not sufficient. Much more important—and more difficult—is the reorientation of habit and attachment. These are affairs of the soul. The goal is to become a *tabula rasa*, an erased wax tablet. Yet, the ideal is not to become open-minded for the sake of individual liberty in and of itself, but for the sake of being susceptible to divine teaching, which is likened here to writing on our hearts. Basil associates this moment of erasure elsewhere with baptism.[19] Baptism is meant to initiate a process in which God rewrites the contents of our minds. It erases our ingrained misconceptions as to what is good for us and what will make us truly happy. In another place, Basil uses the wax image to reiterate the point he makes here about the necessity of unlearning "secular" studies.[20]

It is an interesting ideal, since Basil clearly did *not* forget his own studies. Nor, in other writings, did he counsel other Christians to do so. He famously wrote a piece *To Young Men on the Value of Greek Literature*. In this work, he counsels Christian youths who are studying Greek literature to look for what is beautiful and beneficial in the traditional Greek liberal arts. After all, Moses himself was first trained in Egyptian wisdom before contemplating "He Who Is" (Exod 3:14), and Daniel, living in Babylon, first learned the wisdom of the Chaldeans before devoting himself to the divine teachings (Dan 1:4).[21] To explain the relative merits of divine and Greek teaching, Basil offers the simile of a fruit tree. This tree's proper excellence is to bear fruit. Yet, it is also adorned with foliage, which helps

19. Basil, *On Baptism* 1 (Wagner, 362).

20. Basil, *Hom. Ps.* 32, 7 (Way, 240).

21. Basil, *To Young Men* 2 (D 4:387). Moses' Egyptian education had long been a Christian theme: see Acts 7:22.

to protect it and makes it even more beautiful. Likewise, while the proper pursuit of the soul—its "fruit"—is to attain truth, still the soul can profit from Greek literature. The Greek classics teach many useful doctrines about living wisely and justly in this world. Such study should be viewed as preparatory, as readying one's eyes for the vision of the light itself by showing us the light as if reflected in water.[22]

This suggests that Greek wisdom, though dangerous, does bear reflections of divine teaching. While one must be selective in one's appreciation for Greek literature, it is not a tradition one should look down upon. Moreover, on a practical level, Basil could not have been unaware that Christians had not yet developed methods similar in scope and power to Greek education (*paideia*), which successfully shaped the entire person from an early age in accordance with the norms and values of society. He did try his hand at crafting an exclusively Christian literary curriculum for children entrusted to his monasteries.[23] For his part, however, Basil remained capable of invoking insights from Greek philosophy and literature throughout his career in the church.[24]

Throughout his life, Basil continued to look back on his conversion as principally a conversion *away from* his education, much as he had stated in *ep.* 2. In a letter he wrote in 375 to Eustathius, he describes it as follows:

> Much time had I spent in vanity, and had wasted nearly all my youth in the vain labour which I under-

22. Basil, *To Young Men* 2 (D 4:385).

23. Basil, *LR* 15.3–4; *SR* 292.

24. As he admits in the autobiographical preface to the ascetic works, *On the Faith* (Wagner, 58); more generally, see Ayres and Radde-Gallwitz, "Basil of Caesarea."

> went in acquiring the wisdom made foolish by God (cf. 1 Cor 1:20). Then one day, like someone aroused from a deep sleep, I turned my eyes to the marvellous light of the truth of the Gospel, and I perceived the uselessness of the wisdom *of the princes of this world that are doomed to pass away* (1 Cor 2:6).[25]

Here the "wisdom" he learned in Constantinople and Athens was no reflection of divine illumination, as in *To Young Men*, but rather a "deep sleep" that blinds one to the light. There is no neat and easy way for the reader of Basil to resolve this tension between the two descriptions of Greek *paideia*. In fact, to attempt a reconciliation would be wrongheaded. Basil wrote *To Young Men* and *ep.* 223 in very different contexts for different purposes: the former is meant to encourage young Christians to find what is good and fitting in their studies; the latter seeks to justify himself in the face of accusations against his teaching as a Christian bishop. Basil is consistent in his emphasis upon the need for further illumination beyond Greek wisdom. But he can invoke "Greek wisdom" for very different rhetorical purposes, from exhortation to demonization.

With this ambiguity in mind, let us return to Basil's letter to Gregory (*ep.* 2). Basil associated baptism and conversion with illumination.[26] However, given his own struggles to keep his mind focused on his ascetic vocation, Basil did not believe that this illumination alone was enough for living a life of Christian virtue. We need models. We already noted that Basil found flesh-and-blood models. In his letter to Gregory, Basil also speaks of emulating models

25. Basil, *ep.* 223 (cited from Holmes, *Life Pleasing to God*, 15; cf. D 3:291–93).

26. This association goes back to very early in the church's history: see Heb 6:4 and 10:32; also 2 Cor 3; 4:4–6; Eph 1:18; Justin Martyr, *First Apology* 61, 65.

in the Scriptures, Christianity's own literature. One must come to the Scriptures with a healthy self-knowledge. If chastity is what is lacking, spend some time with the story of Joseph, who resisted the advances of Potiphar's wife; if one needs a lesson in fortitude, consult the story of Job; for each virtue one can find a biblical model. The attention required is likened to representational painting:

> [J]ust as painters in working from models constantly gaze at their exemplar and thus strive to transfer the expression of the original to their own artistry, so too he who is anxious to make himself perfect in all the kinds of virtue must gaze upon the lives of the saints as upon statues, so to speak, that move and act, and must make their excellence his own by imitation.[27]

The notion that one achieves excellence by imitating exemplars was ubiquitous in Basil's day. Often these exemplars were thought to be found in classical literature. Basil's letter is an important example of Christians transferring this to the biblical books. Since at least the time of Origen, the great third-century Christian teacher of Alexandria and Palestine, it was understood that inquiry into difficult theological and doctrinal questions must be guided by scriptural paradigms (*paradeigmata* or *hupodeigmata* in Greek; *exempla* in the Latin translation of Origen). These are biblical passages that are meant to guide the reader's contemplation. So, for instance, one focused one's notions about Christ through meditation on passages such as 1 Corinthians 1:24, where Paul calls him the "power and wisdom of God," and connecting such passages with similar ones, such as the description of divine wisdom in Proverbs 8. We will see that Basil's theology revolves around his interpretation of such passages—phrases that model good

27. Basil, *ep*. 2 (D 1:17).

thinking about God, Christ, and the Spirit. In *ep.* 2, Basil argues that the Christian moral life similarly focuses upon exemplars. The difference is that the exemplars in this context are narratives of biblical characters' lives, which are to be taken as iconic, as "statues that move and act." Much of this would have been seen as commonplace in Basil's day. Whether one modeled oneself on pagan, Jewish, or Christian exemplars, it was assumed that virtue was learned through imitation. The originality of Basil and his contemporaries was to view the biblical heroes as embodying the virtues of Christian renunciation and asceticism, which is by no means a self-evident reading of the texts.[28]

The letter continues with instructions on prayer, which is intended to cultivate the contemplation and "memory" of God. Basil offers further advice on appropriate conversation, dress, eating (once a day, for no longer than an hour) and sleep (light and broken at midnight for prayer). What *ep.* 2 does not mention is the ascetic Christian's need for community. This would become a dominant theme in his subsequent writings on the Christian life. Basil was suspicious of a "go it alone" model of spirituality. For him, to think of ourselves as self-sufficient would be to ignore the many ways in which we need each other, a mutuality that God our Creator intended. Moreover, Christ himself set the example of service-in-community. If you live entirely on our own, Basil asks, "whose feet will you wash?"[29] On our own, it is all too easy to be blind to our own faults. We need the correction and discipline of others to ensure our growth in prayer and penance.

Even at the stage when Basil wrote *ep.* 2, we should not envision him "camping out" along the Iris on his own.

28. For discussion, see Clark, *Reading Renunciation*.

29. Basil, *LR* 5, 7.

It would appear that an inchoate community did form there. We do not know how many there were originally. Gregory of Nazianzus did join him. Most likely so did his brother Gregory of Nyssa. Eustathius would occasionally join them.[30]

Basil did not invent the ascetic life, nor was he the first to bring it to Asia Minor. Naucratius, Macrina, and Eustathius did not await any directions from Basil to live this way. In fact, if we peer behind the evidence, Christians seeking a more devout life show up regularly in Basil's correspondence. In hindsight, we are tempted to think of these figures as "monks" and "nuns," distinct from the more general label "Christians." But this implies a clearer distinction between the two than was apparent, at least in the early years of Basil's career.

During his time in Pontus and continuing after his return to Caesarea in 365, Basil came to assume a position of leadership over groups of particularly devout Christians in these regions. He wrote a number of instructions to guide them. Even before becoming bishop, he composed a document that would be known as the *Small Asceticon*. Rufinus's *Church History* has this to say about Basil during this period before his episcopacy:

> Basil went round the cities and countryside of Pontus and began by his words to rouse that province from its torpor and lack of concern for our hope for the future, kindling it by his preaching, and to banish the insensitivity resulting from long negligence; he compelled it to put away its concern for vain and worldly things and to give its attention to him. He taught people to assemble, to build monasteries, to give time to psalms, hymns, and prayers, to take care of the poor and furnish them with proper housing

30. Basil, *ep*. 223.5.

> and the necessities of life, to establish the way of life of virgins, and to make the life of modesty and chastity desirable to almost everyone.[31]

Rufinus captures well the interconnection of social concern and monastic life that is characteristic of Basil. Also noteworthy is the "public" feel of this mission: Basil sought to preach modesty and chastity to "almost everyone." According to Rufinus, Basil's tour was successful in turning that "dry and barren field" of Pontus into a "luxuriant vineyard" of virtue.[32] One suspects that the groundwork had been laid, to some extent, by Eustathius's own similar efforts. As bishop in Caesarea, a position he occupied from 370 until his death, Basil continued to receive questions from ascetics in Pontus, Cappadocia, and places further east. In response, he expanded his initial work and assembled a collection that would be known as the *Great Asceticon*. At his death, different versions of the work existed in different libraries: one version in Pontus, another in the poorhouse he built as part of the Basileias in Caesarea (about which more in chapter 5). Although one can read Basil's thoughts in translation today as if this were a single work planned out at once, we must remember that the responses we have were written and rewritten throughout Basil's life. The two main components of the *Great Asceticon* as we have it today retain something of their original character, following a question-and-answer format: named after their length, they are the *Shorter Responses* and the *Longer Responses*.[33]

31. Rufinus, *CH* 11.9 (Amidon, 71).

32. Ibid.

33. Although they have traditionally been called Basil's "Rules," they were not so-called originally, and they are in form not rules. For discussion, see Fedwick, *Church and Charisma*, 17–18, 161–65; Rousseau, *Basil of Caesarea*, 191–96, 216–17, 354–59. For response,

There is also a compendium of biblical material known as the *Morals* on matters related to the Christian life. There are also shorter treatises intended to preface the collection and exhort the reader to asceticism.

Traditionally, these have been treated as monastic rules. In fact, they became a classic of the genre. The *Small Asceticon* was translated into Latin by Rufinus in the 390s as the *Regula Basilii*, the "Rule of Basil."[34] This version is cited as recommended reading for monks by St. Benedict in his own enormously influential rule. Some of these monks praised it as sterner than Benedict's.[35] However, Basil did not give his ascetic writings the title of "Rule." The writings evolved over time in response to various queries, and we cannot assume that his audience was always the same. Communal (or coenobitic) monasticism was only taking shape in Asia Minor at this time. While Basil spoke of the need for "renunciation of the world," it is not always clear what this *looked like*, in sociological terms. For instance, we are uncertain to what extent these ascetics were secluded from "the world." As with Eustathius's communities, many of the Christians Basil dealt with lived within or in close proximity to urban areas. It is also clear that there were dual communities, consisting of men and women living side by side, and that the communities included children, some of whom were the offspring of couples who had joined a community together.[36] Yet, there were recognizably "monastic" features to these communities. Each person was assigned a

---

see Silvas, *Asketikon*, 28–30 (esp. n. 20), 102–29, 187 n. 182.

34. For the circumstances, see Silvas, "Edessa to Cassino," 247–59.

35. See Aelfric's *Admonitio*, cited in Corona, *Aelfric's Life*, 45.

36. See Basil, *LR* 15, with Stramara, "Double Monasticism"; Silvas, *Asketikon*, 201 n. 245.

job and there were regular hours of communal prayer and psalm singing.

But perhaps the ambiguity was intentional. As a matter of principle, there was, for Basil, no great distinction between "monastic" and "ordinary" Christianity. Basil viewed asceticism simply as authentic Christianity. It is the form of life centered on Christ's commandments. It is the logical outcome of baptism. In principle, there are not two tiers of Christians—monks and seculars.[37] For Basil, there would be a problem with a Christian who did not seek a more devout life; this would mean spurning Christ's teachings and commands. Basil refused to distinguish a set of "greater" commandments, followed only by a few seeking perfection, from "minor" commandments, incumbent upon all.[38]

37. Rufinus was a notoriously interpretive translator. When he translated Origen's *On First Principles* into Latin, he sometimes "corrected" Origen's doctrines, bringing them in line with Nicene orthodoxy. Rufinus seems to have done something similar with Basil's "rule" as he brought it into his own context, within two decades of Basil's death, in which the line between monks and ordinary baptized Christians was more obvious. He imported into his translation a clear distinction between baptism and monastic profession as two separate, successive phases—a distinction that Basil's Greek text lacks. See Rufinus's *Rule of Basil* 4.3–6 and contrast with *LR* 8 (both in Silvas, *Asketikon*, 187).

38. This distinction was starting to be circulated in Basil's time, especially among Syrian monks. Contrast the anonymous Syriac *Book of Steps* 2.7 (Kitchen and Parmentier, 19–20) with *LR* prol. 2. Although the *Book of Steps* in its current form was not compiled until around 400, it was written earlier, perhaps in Basil's time (though in Syriac in the Persian Empire). For a mid fourth-century date, see Kitchen and Parmentier, xlix-l. Assuming it had travelled to Asia Minor and found Greek adherents, it is possible that Basil knew this teaching and reacted against it. See the comments of Fedwick, "Chronology," 14 n. 81.

For Basil, Christians who ignore the commandments—*any* of them—are unable to see themselves, their world, and their God rightly.[39] Basil speaks of these commandments as divine "illumination." This language of illumination will be of central importance throughout our study of Basil's Trinitarian theology. Its appearance in the *Shorter Responses* (*SR*), which is not in general a work of Trinitarian theology, interestingly invokes the Trinity as well. The questioner in *SR* 1 asks a seemingly odd question: "Is it permissible or fitting for a person to allow himself to do or say whatever he thinks good, without the testimony of the God-inspired scriptures?" In other words, are Christians autonomous moral agents? Can a person substitute private conscience for scriptural testimony? Basil's response unsurprisingly leans toward the negative. He cites Christ's words about the Spirit—"he shall not speak on his own, but will speak whatever he hears" (John 16:13)—and about himself—"I have not spoken on my own; rather, the one who sent me, the Father himself has given me as a commandment what I should speak . . . " (John 12:49). The point is not that Christ and the Spirit carry out these tasks as obedient servants. Basil will go to great lengths in his Trinitarian works to rule out this way of viewing their missions. He is *not* saying, "they are obedient and we should be too." Quite to the contrary, he emphasizes their lordship and our dependence upon Christ and the Spirit. But if our guide, who is in reality Lord, does not act "on his own authority," so to speak, then neither should we. Basil continues:

39. Basil's compendium of the commandments is his *Morals*, where rules are stated and then supported with citations from the NT. Naturally, many commandments are also discussed in the *LR* and *SR*.

> Who then can have attained such a pitch of madness as to dare to conceive on his own so much as a thought when he needs rather the Holy and *Good Spirit as guide for the journey* (cf. Ps 142:10), that he might be *directed into the way of truth* (John 16:13) in thought and words and deeds? For he is blind and dwells in darkness (cf. John 12:35), who is without *the Sun of righteousness* (cf. Mal 4:2), that is our Lord Jesus Christ, who illumines us with his commandments as with rays? For the *commandment of the Lord*, it says, *is bright, illumining the eyes* (Ps 18:9).[40]

One must cultivate a sense of oneself as blind without Christ. Basil adapts the Psalmist's praise of the Torah as illumination, applying it to Christ's teaching and the Good Spirit's guidance.

Basil's vision of monastic life carries many regulations, but for Basil it is merely self-conscious Christianity. The fear of God is not, in his view, an embarrassment or merely a feature of the old covenant, but a pedagogical necessity. He spoke of God as a disciplinarian, likening God to a schoolteacher who occasionally needs to whip his pupils to make them mind.[41] If the severity is distasteful, it worth noting that there were far more severe forms of asceticism among Christians elsewhere, especially in Upper Egypt and Syria. Moreover, Basil did not think that obedience of the commandments was an end in itself. The entire life is rooted first and foremost in love, our natural inclination to the Good, rather than in fear. Moreover, obedience is meant to make us, not slaves, but sons and daughters of God. It should open the Christian to the Trinity, so that he or she can be illuminated and remade in God's image.

40. *SR* 1 (Silvas, *Asketikon*, 273–74, modified); cp. *Morals*, rule 26 (Wagner, 106) and *On the Judgment of God* (Wagner, 42–43).

41. Basil, *hom.* 12.5.

Baptism is a new birth from the Spirit, and this means becoming, to the extent God grants, the very Spirit from which the Christian is born.[42] Christ's commandments are like the signposts marking the journey of this new life. We should not think of the commandments akin to a "to do" list of arbitrary rules; they start with, and grow organically out of, Christ's exhortations to renounce one's possessions and indeed oneself.[43] For Basil, Jesus' call to take up the cross and follow him is not addressed to a narrow few within the church, but to all who bear the name of Christ. One renounces in order to cultivate the love of God and neighbor for which humans are created.

At a time when the boundaries separating the church from the world were becoming fuzzy, when Christianity was becoming the religion of the empire, Basil stood for an older model of church as embodying a call away from the values and mores of society—even if his account of monastic life was itself permeated with traditional Greco-Roman moral philosophy. He could not help but become embroiled in that society, and proved quite adept in political matters. But his heart always remained with his monastic communities. He spoke fondly of the times he could steal away from Caesarea for conferences and all-night vigils with his ascetic friends in Pontus.[44] The survival of his monastic writings in various languages meant that many over the centuries thought of him as first and foremost a monastic regulator. But, as the following chapters will show, his path lay elsewhere, with the public life of

42. Basil, *Morals*, rule 80, cap. 22 (Wagner, 204), based on John 3:6.

43. *LR* 8; *SR* 2.

44. Basil, *ep.* 223; *SR*, prol. 9–11 (Silvas, *Asketikon*, 273, with comments in n. 15).

the church in Caesarea, and particularly with the doctrinal debates that were consuming the broader Christian world and that Basil could not avoid. In his perhaps simplistic rhetoric, baptism entails a life of unquestioning obedience in conformity with the faith. Doctrinal disputes *among the baptized*, therefore, were scandalous to him. They were evidence of moral failure, a point he drives home in the opening lines of his first major doctrinal treatise, *Against Eunomius*:

> If all those upon whom the name of our God and Savior Jesus Christ had been invoked [that is, all the baptized] had preferred not to tamper with the truth of the gospel and to content themselves with the tradition of the apostles and the simplicity of the faith, there would be no need for our present treatise.[45]

Yet there was need for it. As part of his new duties within the church, he had been commanded to write it, perhaps by Eustathius himself, who perceived Eunomius as a grave threat. Each side in this debate believed it had maintained the "simplicity of the faith" to which Basil appeals. We now turn to Eunomius and to Basil's career as interpreter and teacher of the church's public language. Basil had renounced the debating schools of the late Roman rhetorical education system, only to be pulled back into the game through his affiliation with the Christian church.

45. Basil, *Eun.* 1.1 (DelCogliano and Radde-Galwitz [FotC 122], 81); cf. *On the Judgment of God* (Wagner, 37–38).

TWO

Eunomius: Basil's Opponent and His Context

Basil was baptized into a church that was increasingly polarized over its teaching. We will begin our study of his response by meeting some of the major players in the debates of the 350s and 360s, placing Eunomius's first major work, which Basil would counter in his *Against Eunomius*, within this context. Naturally, in a short survey, we must simplify what is a complicated story.

Homoians, Homoiousians, and Nicenes

With Constantius II on the imperial throne, the 350s saw a series of councils in the East and the West. The unintended result was disunity, especially in the East—even among former allies. Before speaking of the split, we must set some background. Probably the most iconic event in the fourth-century Trinitarian controversies is the condemnation of Arius at the Council of Nicaea in 325. At least in the eyes of his opponents, Arius had erred in making the Son foreign to the Father in being and subsequent to the Father in time (rather than coeternal). In declaring the Son to be "of the same substance" (*homoousios*) as the Father and "from the substance of the Father," the Nicene Creed has been seen as setting the agenda of the fourth century as anti-Arian. With Nicaea standing out as the leading event, it has appeared to many that the great enemy of fourth-century Christian faith was "Arian" subordinationism—which would include any theology that portrays the Son as inferior to God. To be sure, especially in the years following 350, there were those at the times who saw things in exactly this way. Athanasius of Alexandria is a prime example of a theologian and bishop whose fundamental rallying cry, especially in the 350s, was Nicaea and its anti-Arianism. However, many at the time viewed Arius as little more than a minor annoyance. The real threat, as they perceived it, lay in the ideas of Marcellus of Ancyra.

Marcellus's theology is complicated and difficult to reconstruct from the surviving documents, all of which are hostile to him. Like many others, even some of his opponents, he was present at Nicaea and signed its creed. He perceived a strong unity between God and the Word, so much so that he was interpreted as too closely comparing the two to a human mind and its word. He did not view them as independent realities. Moreover, he denied that the title "Son" applies to the Word before the incarnation, which led to further suspicion that he was reviving Sabellianism or Monarchianism, heresies of the second and third centuries that did not view the Son as eternally distinct from the Father. The ostracism of Marcellus was not universal. The paradigmatic supporter of Nicaea, Athanasius, was friendly towards him and never rejected him. Marcellus's own community in Ancyra remained loyal to him even after his death. But many in the East felt differently. This broad grouping of anti-Marcellans, an alliance that persisted in various forms from the 330s through the 350s, has been dubbed the "Eusebians" after two leading bishops, Eusebius of Caesarea and Eusebius of Nicomedia. Certainly not all Christians associated with the group thought alike. But a common anti-Sabellianism (i.e., anti-Marcellanism) united them. This tradition is crucial for our study, since it was a formative influence on Basil throughout his career, even as the nature of the alliance associated with it changed drastically.

It began to change in the final years of the 350s, when Basil was newly baptized and seeking to live in tranquility alongside the Iris, far removed from these debates. Towards the end of the decade, the cohesion of the "Eusebian" alliance began to unravel. Two events were pivotal: out of them two distinct parties—the Homoians and the Homoiousians—emerged from the old alliance. First, in 357, a council was held in Sirmium in Pannonia (part of modern Serbia), out of which came a creed condemning all uses of "substance" (*substantia* in Latin; *ousia* in Greek) in confessions of faith, singling out two positions in particular: that the Son is "the same in substance" (*homoousios*) as the Father, and that he is "of like substance" (*homoiousios*).[1] That is, Sirmium set itself against the Nicene confession and the emerging Homoiousian movement. Although Sirmium sought to lump the Homoiousians together with the Nicenes, in fact, the Homoiousians came out of the broadly Eusebian, anti-Marcellan tradition.

Sirmium's opponents called the creed the "Blasphemy of Sirmium." To its supporters, the creed was a party

1. It is best preserved by Hilary of Poitiers, *On the Synods*.

"manifesto."[2] We call this emerging party the Homoians, since they affirmed merely that the Son is "like" (*homoios*) the Father, while avoiding substance language. At Sirmium, the party was led by the bishops Germinus, Valens (not to be confused with the emperor), Ursacius, and George of Alexandria (Athanasius's replacement since 351). There are other important names to associate with the Homoian party. Acacius succeeded the great historian and theologian Eusebius as bishop of Caesarea Maritima in Palestine. Eudoxius was bishop of Germanica, but was transferred in 358 to Antioch and in 360 to Constantinople. The orbit of his influence reached the imperial level. He will become important for our story as a patron of Eunomius, at least for a few crucial years. Another leading Homoian was Euzoius, who would be placed on the episcopal throne at Antioch in 361 to replace Eudoxius after his initial replacement, Meletius, proved unacceptable to the Homoians. We will return to the problems in Antioch shortly.

The other pivotal event was a synod of bishops in Ancyra summoned in 358 by Basil of Ancyra. This synod witnessed the consolidation of the Homoiousians into an identifiable grouping. Like his fellow Homoiousians, Basil of Ancyra's doctrinal résumé was strongly Eusebian. He was the replacement for Marcellus as bishop of Ancyra when Marcellus was ousted from that office by the Eusebians in 336. Basil of Ancyra had attended the decidedly Eusebian dedication council in Antioch in 341 and signed the Eusebian Macrostich creed. He had debated Marcellus's disciple Photinus at a Council in Sirmium in 351 and ensured his condemnation. But Basil was alarmed by events in Antioch in the late 350s, in particular the radical Homoian doctrines of Aetius, to whom Eudoxius

2. Hanson, *Search*, 347.

was giving aid and succor. He had been tipped off to these events by a letter written by George of Laodicea, another Eusebian. George interpreted Aetius as teaching that the Son is "unlike" (*anhomoios*) the Father—thus leading to the label of radical Homoian theology as "Anhomoian."

The Synod of Ancyra issued a lengthy and theologically rich statement, which was written by Basil.[3] Another letter from around the time of the synod, written by George in collaboration with Basil and the others, defended the use of *ousia* over against Homoian attacks. George's letter anticipates aspects of Basil of Caesarea's theology.[4] Other prominent Homoiousians included Basil's mentor Eustathius and Macedonius of Constantinople (the latter's participation led fifth-century historians to call the group "Macedonians").[5] The heresiologist Epiphanius preserved the documents of the Homoiousians. But he quite unfairly labeled them as "Semi-Arians." The label has stuck, unfortunately, and it is has fueled the perception that there was a significant fight starting in 358 between the Homoiousians

3. For its influence on Basil of Caesarea's understanding of theological language, see DelCogliano, *Basil's Anti-Eunomian Theory*, 182–84.

4. For passages that sound (in hindsight) very much like Basil of Caesarea, see, e.g., "Letter of George" *apud* Epiphanius, *Panarion* 73.16.2 and 73.16.5–6.

5. The label "Macedonian" has often been used more restrictively by modern historians, as a synonym for the "Pneumatomachians" (or "Spirit-fighters"), especially in the 380s. The fifth-century historians use it as a name for the Homoiousian party even as early as the Council of Constantinople in 360: see Socrates, *CH* 2.45; 3.25; 4.1, 4; Sozomen, *CH* 4.26–27. They do so because of the influence of Macedonius on the Homoiousian coalition, particularly after the removal of many members of this coalition from their sees at Constantinople in 360; Macedonius himself was deposed there. This should not be taken as evidence that the label "Macedonian" was used for Homoiousians in the 360s.

and the Homoousian Nicenes such as Athanasius (who were staunchly opposed to any and all "Arianism"). Since the eighteenth-century historian Edward Gibbon wrote in his *History of the Decline and Fall of the Roman Empire* that the Trinitarian controversy was really over a diphthong (that is, over the difference between *oi* and *o*), it has become cliché to report that there was an extended fight between these two parties. The closeness of their confessional formulae, which was supposedly lost on fourth-century partisans, is supposed to underscore the ridiculousness of the entire controversy. Like many truisms one hears about the fourth century, this one is false. Fourth-century authors as different as Athanasius, Eunomius, and Basil recognized that the two formulae functionally mean the same, when rightly interpreted. More importantly, the contemporary opponent against whom the Homoiousians were fighting was the Homoian party, especially its radical wing, not the Nicene party. George died by 360 and Basil of Ancyra around 363. As we will see, around this time, leading Homoiousians in Antioch and Asia Minor began successfully seeking reconciliation with the Nicene party, particularly in the West. For his part, the staunchly Nicene Athanasius sought a common front with them beginning in 359. To be sure, the two sides were coming from different backgrounds, with the Homoiousians originating as fierce anti-Marcellans and Athanasius as a friend of Marcellus. However, they did not allow this to undermine their common interest in opposing the Homoians.

In 359, Constantius sought to end the bickering by holding simultaneous, twin councils: one in the West at Ariminum (modern Rimini, Italy), the other in the East at Seleucia in Isauria (southeastern Asia Minor). Neither council went as planned. In the end Constantius had to engineer the acceptance of a Homoian creed. This creed, known as the Creed of Niké (after the city in which Constantius resolved the issue), outlawed the use of *ousia* in formal confessions of faith and declared that the Son is "like the Father as the scriptures teach." Another popular way of phrasing the Son's likeness was offered by Acacius at Seleucia: he is like the Father "in will, but not in essence." In January 360, a smaller council was held in Constantinople to confirm this creed and to eliminate the opposition (it is not to be confused with the council held there in 381 which produced the Creed many of us are familiar with). The council closed on February 15 with the consecration of the church of Holy Wisdom (Hagia Sophia); this is the church that would be rebuilt by Justinian in its current, magnificent form.[6] At the council, Acacius presided over approximately fifty bishops. Many Homoiousian bishops were deposed from their sees, some of them on behavioral rather than doctrinal charges. As a sign of its moderation, the council also deposed Aetius, who was too radical for Acacius. The leading Homoian, Eudoxius, who had been ousted from Antioch by a previous council, was installed as bishop of Constantinople. Control of the Eastern capital gave Eudoxius a tremendous opportunity for influence. There, in 366, he baptized Emperor Valens into Homoian Christianity, an event that would prove momentous for Basil as bishop of Caesarea—but that is to skip ahead. Perhaps the most important act of the 360 Council of Constantinople for our story is that it installed Eunomius as bishop of Cyzicus.

A young Basil of Caesarea was also present at the council, with his younger brother Gregory. It is unclear in what capacity he attended or why—perhaps he simply

6. Socrates, *CH* 2.43.

wanted to see the new church of Holy Wisdom, which had not yet been erected during his time there as a student. What is clear is that he occupied no high office in the church yet. He had been baptized, but was at most a lector in the church. His bishop, Dianius, attended and, to Basil's dismay, signed its confession of faith. On his deathbed two years later, he assured Basil that he had done so only "in the simplicity of his heart," without fully understanding what he was signing. Basil left the council at some point before its conclusion. Willingly or not, he had waded into the Church's stormy controversies over Christ and his relation to God.

Eunomius's Theology: The Unbegotten God and the Teaching of Christ

Although Eunomius came off a winner in 360, he ultimately had the bad fortune of being repeatedly condemned and exiled. Even today it is difficult to get a fully accurate picture of his teaching, despite the survival of some of his writings. Yet, it is crucial to make an attempt at reconstructing Eunomius's thought if we are to make sense of Basil. We have Eunomius's *Apology* (360), the work that Basil responded to in his *Against Eunomius* (364/65). We also have many quotations from his second defense, amusingly titled *Apology for the Apology* (379–80). This work, published around the time of Basil's death, was refuted by Gregory of Nyssa in his *Against Eunomius* (380–81/82); we can reconstruct Eunomius's *Apology for the Apology* from the quotations in Gregory's work alone. Finally, we have a brief *Confession of Faith* (383) and a number of fragments quoted by later authors. Eunomius was evidently a powerful thinker whose mind ranged over major topics in Christian doctrine—the nature of God, the person and work of Christ, and the Holy Spirit. Here, we will analyze the first two topics, leaving his teaching on the Spirit for chapter 4.

It is the polemic of Basil and others that has given us the caricature of Eunomius as a "rationalist" more concerned with logical niceties than with Christian piety. Basil tried his hand at character assassination, and Eunomius repaid the favor in the *Apology for the Apology*. But, since we are fortunate to have him in his own words, we can try to peer behind this polemic and see what was motivating him. His *Apology*, as the title suggests, was a defense. He offered it, so it appears, at the Council of Constantinople in 360. Eunomius had most likely been accused of teaching that the Son is unlike the Father in all respects. His defense might strike us as too clever by half, as he argued that God is not like *anything*, since in his essence God is absolutely incomparable. But apparently it worked. As noted earlier, thanks to the machinations of Eudoxius, he was elevated to the office of bishop and installed in the see of Cyzicus.[7] This was no small feat, since the very same council deposed his teacher, Aetius.

Once we scratch beneath the *Apology*'s bombastic surface, we might find Eunomius's account of Christian doctrine more sympathetic. The *Apology* begins with an appeal to the audience not to give heed to the opinions of the majority—Eunomius knew well that, even with the support of notable Homoians, his ideas might appear eccentric—but to "the teaching of our Savior Jesus Christ."[8] The role of Christ as the teacher and revealer *par excellence* is of the utmost important for Eunomius. Christ himself

7. Eudoxius was transferred from Antioch, where he had been bishop of the Homoian Christians since 358, to Constantinople.

8. *Apol.* 2 (Vaggione, 37).

gave us the titles by which we contemplate him and his Father.[9] Eunomius is notorious for his claim that we can know the essence (or substance—a synonym in the following pages) of God, and that this knowledge can be summarized with the title "Unbegotten." This strikes the modern reader as peculiar, and upon reading Eunomius's dizzying rationale for how this name denotes the simple essence of God, the puzzle might only increase.[10] However, we must bear in mind that for Eunomius human knowledge of God is grounded ultimately in Christ's teaching. This is perhaps clearest in Eunomius's response to Basil. For Basil, the divine substance is unknowable. Eunomius responded in the *Apology for the Apology* not by stressing the powers of the human mind to know God, but by emphasizing Christ's role as revealer. If Christ cannot reveal God's very essence to us, then

> it is in vain that he names himself "Door," since there would be no one going in to understand and contemplate the Father; in vain also "Way," if he provides no opportunity for those who desire to come to the Father; and how would he be Light, if he did not illuminate people, if he did not shine upon the mind's eye so that it may perceive himself and the transcendent Light?[11]

Here is the same language of illumination that will be central for Basil. By anchoring doctrine in the teaching of Christ, Eunomius was following Origen and the

9. *AA*, cited at G. Nyssa, *Eun.* 2.295; 2.351.

10. I have attempted to clarify Eunomius's arguments regarding divine simplicity and the title "Unbegotten" in Radde-Gallwitz, *Basil, Gregory, and Transformation*, 87–112.

11. *AA*, quoted at G. Nyssa, *Eun.* 3.8.5 (trans. by Stuart G. Hall, in *Gregory of Nyssa: Contra Eunomium III*, edited by Johan Leemans).

entire early Christian tradition. But his use of this tradition was unique. One might reasonably ask, *how* exactly does Christ reveal God's essence to us, and in particular, where is it said that "Unbegotten" is the unique title of this essence? Eunomius does not claim that this term appears in the Bible.[12] But "Only-Begotten" is a biblical title of the Son of God. And we need a term that marks the fundamental *difference* between the two—a term which secures the incomparabililty of the God of the universe. It helps that, by Eunomius's time, the habit of using the term "Unbegotten" for God was deeply ingrained in Christian tradition. But Eunomius also presents it as part of the common notion of God that any reasonable human being would recognize. It is simply a way of saying that God is one and that there is no source "before" God from which God comes into being.[13] God is the "One Who Is" (Exod 3:14), not the one who comes into being.[14] This is not true of the Son, who is begotten by the Father.

To explain his emphasis on the difference between God and Christ, we must look to how he interpreted a few verses. We will begin with one of his favorites, 1 Corinthians 8:6:

> But for us there is one God, the Father, from whom
> are all things and for whom we are,

12. Eunomius does once insert the word into a quotation 1 Cor 8:6 (*Apol.* 25). While there is one precedent for this reading in earlier Christian literature, it seems that Eunomius is consciously glossing the verse, rather than claiming that the word "unbegotten" was actually in the text. The precedent occurs in the "Letter to Flora" by the second-century "Valentinian" teacher Ptolemy: preserved in Epiphanius, *Panarion* 33.7.6. There is no reason to suspect that Eunomius drew on Ptolemy.

13. *Apol.* 7.

14. On Exod 3:14 as offering the divine name, see *Apol.* 17.

> And one Lord, Jesus Christ, though whom are all things and through whom we are.

Notice the similarity between this verse and the brief "creed" that Eunomius quotes at the beginning of the doctrinal section of the *Apology*:

> We believe in one God, the Father almighty, from whom are all things;
>
> And in one only-begotten Son of God, God the Word, our Lord Jesus Christ, through whom are all things;
>
> And in one holy Spirit, the Counsellor, in whom is given to each of the saints an apportionment of every grace according to measure for the common good.[15]

For Eunomius, the prepositions are important: *from* whom, *through* whom, *in* whom. God is the ultimate, unoriginated origin of all; the Son is the mediator; and the Spirit is the one in whom "the saints" receive God's blessings. Also important is that there is *one* of each: one God, one Lord, one Spirit. Each is distinct and there is no sharing of nature among them.

A key testimony for Eunomius was Christ's saying in John 17:3: "This is eternal life, that they know you, the only

15. *Apol.* 5 (Vaggione, 39). It is important to note that the creed Eunomius offers is not itself controversial, or at least that it admits of multiple interpretations that could be acceptable to the various parties of the fourth century. In responding to it, Basil mocks Eunomius for trying to supplement it with his own peculiar emphasis upon God's unbegotten character. He does not attack the wording of the creed itself. Basil does note that some have claimed that Eunomius's creed goes back to Arius; Basil repeats the claim, but neither explicitly endorses it nor uses it to discredit the creed's content; see *Eun.* 1.4. In this section, Basil even refers to it as "the faith of the fathers" and "the pious tradition of the fathers" (though he does so in order to underscore the differences between the creed and Eunomius's own theology).

true God, and Jesus Christ, whom you sent." Christ himself prays here, on his disciples' behalf, to the "only true God." While Christ is *their* Lord and God, he acknowledges the only true God as not only his Father, but as his God.[16] Christ is thus a mediator between God and the world, not just as God-in-flesh (as Basil would maintain), but in his very being. According to Eunomius, this is why Jesus proclaimed in John 14:28 that the Father who sent him is "greater" than he is.[17] While "greater" might suggest a comparison of "degrees," in fact Eunomius's fundamental argument throughout the *Apology* is that *the Unbegotten God is in his essence incomparable*, not only to the world but also to the only-begotten Son.[18] If this point is granted, then claiming that the Son is "like the Father in essence" (*homoios kat' ousian*, the position of the Homoiousians) will be shown to be impious and illogical.[19] Nothing can be *like* in essence to that which is in essence incomparable. Eunomius was less worried about what for him was the obviously erroneous Nicene confession that the Son is equal or the same as the Father in essence (*homoousion*). To him this clearly contradicts John 14:28, and has Sabellianism as its logical consequence.

But a significant problem remains for Eunomius. How are we to interpret descriptions that are used in the Bible for both God and the Son, or for both God and the created world? Eunomius quite reasonably claims that words like "eye" are only metaphorically applied to God. But what about "light," "life," and "power"? In addition to naming

16. In John 20:17, which is quoted by Eunomius in both *Apol.* 21 and *AA* (*apud* G. Nyssa, *Eun.* 3.9.61, discussed at length in 3.10).

17. See *Apol.* 11.

18. Stated most clearly in *Apol.* 11 and 26.

19. See esp. *Apol.* 18.

created phenomena, these words are used of the Father and the Son. Is God-as-light different from the Son-as-light? His answer is that "just as the unbegotten differs from the begotten, so 'the light' must differ from 'the light.'"[20] That is, even though similar terms are used for the Son as for God, God remains incomparable *even with respect to those terms*. Merely sharing titles does not mean they share the same essence. Rather, their incomparability in essence implies that they bear these titles in different ways, just like a lamp and the sun can both be called lights, despite their vastly different natures.

A final noteworthy feature of Eunomius's theology, and in particular his Christology, is his emphasis upon the unity of Christ. Everyone accepted that there was a wide variety of descriptions of Christ in the scriptures. Consider, for example, Proverbs 8:22, where Wisdom—interpreted as Christ by the early Christians—is said to have been created. Yet, the Word of God is also the one "through whom all things were created" (John 1:3; compare 1 Cor 8:6). Moreover, he himself is Lord and God. Some theologians, most notoriously Athanasius, had proposed that we must draw a distinction between those passages that refer to the Word in his incarnate state and those that refer to his eternal being. Eunomius would have none of this kind of division. For him, the various verses tell a coherent story. God first creates or begets (the words are equivalent for Eunomius) the Son, who is the "firstborn of all creation." In turn, through the Son, God creates the Spirit and all else. So, the Son is created, though he is not in the same class as the other creatures. Eunomius believes that the Son became flesh. But this does not mean that we say that the "making" referred to in Proverbs 8:22 or Acts 2:36 are

20. *Apol.* 19 (Vaggione, 59).

descriptions of his incarnation, as Athanasius believed. For Eunomius, these passages refer to his creation by God before the ages. In his incarnate life, Jesus taught us about his God and Father in such a way that we would be clear about their essential *differences.* In so doing, Christ became the "firstborn of many brothers" (Rom 8:29), the leader of the chorus of voices praising his God and ours, his Father and ours.[21] In his understanding of God as the Unbegotten, and hence incomparable, essence, as well as in his Christology and pneumatology (about which more in chapter 4), Eunomius provided the whetstone that sharpened Basil's earliest extensive theological writing.

The Historical Context of Basil's Reply

By the time Basil replied to Eunomius, he was a supporter of the Nicene faith. In hindsight, this might seem obvious, but at the time, it was far from it. Outside of a handful of areas, most notably Rome and Athanasius's circle in Alexandria, the Nicene position was not terribly popular in 360. In some places throughout the preceding decade it appears to have been relatively unknown. The most famous promoter of Nicaea, Athanasius of Alexandria, was in exile (for the third time) from 356 to 362. He was in that time, as always, writing prolifically. His writing was now explicitly and extensively devoted to defending Nicaea's catchphrases that the Son is "of the same substance" (*homoousion*) as the Father and "from the substance of the Father" (*ek tēs tou patros ousias*). A rival bishop had been installed in Alexandria—George, a Cappadocian by birth and a radical Homoian who supported Aetius and Eunomius. The Nicene cause might have looked bleak. However, moves

21. See Basil's comments in *Eun.* 2.23 on the use of Rom 8:29.

were being made to bring Homoiousians and Nicenes together. Between 359 and 361, Athanasius, typically a fiery polemicist, wrote a work *On the Synods*, which, along with its anti-Homoian argumentation, had the irenic intent of showing that the Homoiousian position logically equates to the Nicene.

Both groups had a common front in opposing the Homoians, especially the more radical ones like Eunomius. However, efforts at bringing Homoiousians and Nicenes together were complicated both by longstanding theological differences and by the closely related question of who was in communion with whom. It is important to remember that the fourth-century church was a federation or network of episcopal sees. Mutual recognition by bishops ensured legitimacy. Any bishop felt it important to have one's peers recognize him as in communion with them, but it mattered most of all for holders of the major sees like Alexandria and Antioch. We have seen that there were two claimants in Alexandria, the Homoian George and the Nicene Athanasius. In 362, a pagan mob lynched George and paraded his corpse around the city on a camel. This did not stop the Homoians from proposing Lucius as his successor, prolonging the schism there.

There was an even more complicated dispute over the see of Antioch. The old-school Nicenes supported Paulinus, who had been consecrated in 362 by a radical supporter of Nicaea from the West, Lucifer of Cagliari. The Homoians had placed Eudoxius on the throne of Antioch in 358. But in 360 he was transferred to Constantinople. Meletius was made bishop of Antioch in his place. However, he proved an unreliable ally for the Homoians, since his preaching seemed to veer in the Homoiousian direction. By 361, he was deposed. The Homoians proposed Euzoius as his replacement, but not all recognized him as legitimate. This meant that, from 362 until 379, there were three separate communities in Antioch, centered on three different men claiming to be bishop: Paulinus (the Nicene, supported by Athanasius and by Rome), Meletius (popular in Syria and Asia Minor among the Homoiousians, including Basil of Caesarea), and Euzoius (the Homoian, who had imperial support under Valens). Clearly, at least two camels would be needed to settle matters in Antioch. We will return to the Antiochene schism in chapter 8.

Efforts to bridge divisions continued. When the Emperor Constantius died in 361, the Homoians lost a powerful patron. His successor, Julian, converted to paganism after being raised a Christian; Christian tradition has labeled him "the Apostate." In an effort to foment confusion and division among Christians, Julian pronounced an amnesty on exiled bishops. Meletius returned to Antioch. Athanasius returned to Alexandria, where he called a council in 362, which issued the *Tome to the Antiochenes*, a document aiming to resolve the Homoiousian-Nicene impasse in Antioch. In 363, Julian died in battle against the Persians. His successor, Jovian, lived only a year, but in it a significant event happened.[22] At Antioch a synod of Homoiousian bishops assembled together, surprisingly, with one of the leading Homoians, Acacius of Caesarea. The synod expressed its support for the Nicene Creed. The bishops affirmed that the Son is "of the same substance" (*homoousion*) as the Father, suggesting that this confession secures three essential points: (1) that the Son is "from the Father's substance"; (2) that the Son is like the Father in substance, that is, they assumed that the Nicene and the

22. This event is narrated in Socrates, *CH* 3.25; and Sozomen, *CH* 6.4.

Homoiousian positions are identical; and (3) that the heresy of Arius, recently revived by those who teach the Son's *unlikeness* to the Father, is to be rejected. This last point was directed against Eunomius and the radical Homoians. Among those who signed the document were two figures of great importance for Basil's career: Meletius of Antioch, the bishop whom Basil supported in the schism there, and Eusebius of Samosata, who would later ensure Basil's consecration as bishop.

In 364, Valentinian, a supporter of Nicaea, assumed the purple. For co-emperor he chose his brother, Valens, who favored Homoian Christianity. In the same year, a synod of Homoiousian bishops was held at Lampsacus, on the Asiatic coast of the Hellespont. This group rejected the Council of Constantinople of 360, setting themselves firmly against Eudoxius and his party. They reaffirmed the Second Creed of the Dedication Council of Antioch (341), a crucial Eusebian confession.[23] The alliance struck there paved the way for further developments. Around this time, the Homoiousians decided to pursue communion with Rome and thus assented to the Nicene Creed. They sent a delegation of three bishops—one of which was Eustathius of Sebasteia—to Rome, where mutual communion was recognized by Pope Liberius (352–66) and the delegates.[24] After returning home, Eustathius and other Homoiousians held a council at Tyana in 367, at which Basil himself might have been present.[25] Plans for another, more universal council in Tarsus were made, but thwarted by Eudoxius,

23. See Socrates, *CH* 4.2, 4; Sozomen, *CH* 6.7.

24. See Socrates, *CH* 4.12; Sozomen, *CH* 6.10–11.

25. For Tyana, see Sozomen, *CH* 6.12. For the conjecture of Basil's presence, see Rousseau, *Basil*, 101 n. 17; and Silvas, *Asketikon*, 95–96, both of whom pick up on a suggestion made by Dom Gribomont.

who prompted Emperor Valens to nix it. But important groundwork had been laid for a new alliance between Nicenes and Homoiousians.

Meanwhile, Eunomius did not fare well in Cyzicus. Our sources are murky, but it appears not to have been a week before he got himself into trouble. Consecrated in Constantinople on January 2 or 3, 360, he gave his inaugural sermon in Cyzicus at the feast of the Theophany (which Westerners call Epiphany) on January 6.[26] The clergy in Cyzicus would have none of him. They complained to Eudoxius in Constantinople. Even Emperor Constantius got involved. At some point, Eunomius left Cyzicus and returned to his native Cappadocia. Eunomius would never hold episcopal office again. However, this "failure" provided an opportunity of sorts. Eunomius broke with Eudoxius, who refused to honor a promise to restore Aetius. Aetius had moved to Lesbos, where the Emperor Julian had given him land (due to a mutual friendship). Now living on his own property in Chalcedon, Eunomius rejoined forces with his teacher. It might be going too far to say that around this time the two started their own "sect."[27] But they did ordain likeminded bishops and presbyters in a small, alternative church that survived well into the fifth century. Eunomius fell foul of the new emperor Valens when he supported the usurper Procopius; Valens ordered his exile, but soon allowed him to return. In 366 Aetius died. In 370 Eudoxius followed, with Demophilus succeeding him as Homoian bishop of Constantinople. Eunomius was banished to exile on the island of Naxos in the Aegean Sea, where he would

26. Such is the reconstruction of events offered by Vaggione, *Eunomius*, 231 n. 216.

27. As the fifth-century Nicene historian Theodoret claims in *CH* 2.30.11.

stay until exiles were allowed to return in 378. From Naxos, Eunomius was silent. There is more to his story, but that is to jump ahead.

It is within the milieu of Homoiousians allying themselves with Nicenes in the 360s that we must place Basil early in his career.[28] It is noteworthy that members of this alliance typically cemented their bonds of communion by renouncing the doctrines of Aetius, Eunomius, and Eudoxius. Throughout his entire career, Basil remained a theologian who spoke Nicene with a Homoiousian accent. Not only did he continue to speak of the Son as "like the Father in substance," but he also viewed Marcellan "Sabellianism" as a threat throughout his career, even as he carried forward the strong Homoiousian suspicion of Eunomius. Moreover, the alliances he formed with

28. Perhaps before his ordination, Basil had written to ask Apollinarius of Laodicea about the term *homoousion* (*ep.* 361). Apollinarius would later become notorious for advocating that Christ had no human mind, only the divine Logos. But at this stage, he should be viewed simply as a staunch advocate of Nicaea. We have Apollinarius's reply to Basil (*ep.* 362; see also *epp.* 363 and 364). Here, he specifies that "substance" is not to be understood in various inappropriate senses—it is not, for instance, a material "stuff" shared by Father and Son. We are unsure how deeply Apollinarius influenced Basil. Basil's *ep.* 361 reveals him to be skeptical about the term, preferring to say that the Son is "invariably like the Father in essence with no difference." But how he describes this sounds very much like his later understanding of Nicaea: "For we have supposed that whatever by way of hypothesis the substance of the Father is assumed to be, this must by all means be assumed as also that of the Son" (D 4:335). The example Basil offers of such a shared essential property is "light." During Basil's later dispute with Eustathius, beginning in 372, the latter will accuse Basil of Sabellianism because of his correpondence with Apollinarius (whom Eustathius presumably thought was Sabellian). See *ep.* 223 for Basil's later reflections on this early correspondence.

Eustathius and Meletius shaped the development of his thinking.

Many scholars have viewed the movement of Homoiousians allying themselves with Nicenes through cynical lenses. They couldn't *really* have meant it. Wouldn't that mean capitulation to the other side? Since this alliance was so influential on the eventual acceptance of the Nicene faith, some critics of that doctrine have sought to discredit it by showing it owes its origins to (gasp) the Homoiousians. Unfortunately, this cynical line of interpretation is based on rather blindly accepting certain ancient documents, such as Epiphanius's writings, which refer to the Homoiousians as "Semi-Arians." This was never an impartial or particularly accurate depiction, and it only was meant to name the party circa 358–59, that is, before the efforts at reconciliation that we have outlined got underway. Once we refuse this label, we see that the alliance that Basil inherited was not an amalgam of irreconcilable foes, but a practical attempt at Christian unity over against the Homoians, who were perceived as a real threat, especially under Constantius and later Valens when they enjoyed imperial support. It is not, of course, that everyone who entered into the alliance did so with full sincerity. The cynics can certainly point to Eustathius as a great example of someone who seems to have reneged on his commitment to Nicaea. But it would be wrongheaded to assume that Eustathius represented the norm. Indeed, Basil, who clearly came out of the same background, later berated Eustathius for his duplicity. But Basil did not extend his suspicion to others, such as Meletius of Antioch, who had moved in the direction of Nicaea. Nor, it seems, should we, unless we are presented with reasons for doing so.

THREE

The Theology of the Only-Begotten Son (*Against Eunomius* 1–2)

Basil had become disillusioned with his bishop, Dianius, for signing the Council of Constantinople's confession in 360. Upon returning home from the council, Basil, still merely a lector in the church, retreated from public church life in Caesarea, taking up his ascetic vocation in Annisa for a second time. However, he returned to Caesarea in 362 to attend Dianius on his deathbed. Dianius's replacement, Eusebius, ordained Basil as presbyter (from which our word "priest" comes). This would bring new duties, no doubt including participation at the Eucharist on the four times a week it was held in Caesarea: Sunday, Wednesday, Friday, and Saturday.[1] Shortly after his ordination, however, Basil and Eusebius had a falling out, over what we do not know. For a third time, Basil made for Annisa, where he

1. Or, as Basil calls them, "the Lord's Day, the Fourth Day, Preparation, and Sabbath" (*ep.* 93).

spent eighteen months stretching from 363 to 365, again devoting himself to the "philosophical life." But he could not escape church affairs.

It was most likely during this time that he was twice asked to write on the doctrinal matters rocking the church. One of these requests prompted his three books *Against Eunomius*, which we will investigate in some depth shortly. The other is also worth mentioning. In his *ep.* 9, to a certain Maximus the philosopher, Basil offers his first explicit defense of the Nicene dogma. For him the heart of the Creed is the language of "light from light" and "true God from true God": "Now no one can possibly conceive of any variation either of light in relation to light, or truth to truth, or of the substance of the Only-Begotten to that of the Father."[2] Basil offers a very different interpretation of the shared titles of Father and Son than we have seen in Eunomius, who was clearly able to conceive of variation between the light and the light. For Basil, the sharing of titles by Father and Son shows that their substances are not different at all. It is noteworthy that the point is phrased in the negative: "no one can possibly conceive" of the Son as truly different from the Father in light, divinity, or substance.

In *Against Eunomius*, Basil elaborates the same understanding of the Father-Son relationship at greater length. In the opening chapter, he says he has been commanded to write it.[3] While we cannot be certain, it is quite likely that Basil is referring to a request from Eustathius, and that the work was drawn up in preparation for the synod at Lampsacus.[4] *Against Eunomius* is a remarkable work and the only surviving treatise of any theological depth from

2. *Ep.* 9 (D 1:97–99).

3. *Eun.* 1.1.

4. Assuming that this is the work Basil refers to in *ep.* 223.

this moment in the mid 360s, when the Homoiousian and Nicene parties were coming together. Basil's purpose is simple: to refute Eunomius. To that end, he employs a method of writing that Origen had used in his refutation to the pagan Celsus's criticism of Christianity: he cites a portion of his opponent's text and then comments on and argues against this passage. While he does not quote the entire *Apology*, his choices are not purely malicious. Polemical motivations are never far below the surface; yet, there is some attempt to understand Eunomius before criticizing.

The work is a piece of judicial oratory: Basil wants us to read it as if we are jurors hearing Eunomius's defense and finding it woefully deficient. At times, Basil believes, Eunomius's fraud is plain; he only needs to cite Eunomius's words to expose it. Other times, Basil claims that Eunomius has cloaked his real intentions, and so lengthy discussions of Eunomius's treacherous arguments are needed. In describing Eunomius, Basil is not above casting suspicion worthy of a conspiracy theorist: "I think everything he says is part of his plot."[5]

Still, this is a serious theological work, the first of Basil's career. It responds to the dogmatic disputes of his day, while penetrating to the inner meaning of the various confessions. Although he offers no explicit defense of Nicaea, he once uses the term *homoousion* in its technical sense. He argues that the Son's consubstantiality is implied when Hebrews 1:3 calls him the "character of God's being [*hypostasis*]."[6] Also, he once uses other language from the

5. *Eun.* 1.4. All quotations of this work are taken from DelCogliano and Radde-Gallwitz (FotC 122), unless otherwise indicated.

6. *Eun.* 1.20. The word *hypostasis* would later have a technical significance for Basil, which it did not yet carry in *Against Eunomius.*

Nicene Creed, describing the Son as proceeding "from [God the Father's] substance."[7] Elsewhere in the work, he continues to use "likeness in substance."[8] He is responding to Eunomius, for whom the Homoiousian formula is unacceptable, in part because it equates to the (absurd) Nicene formula. Basil seems to grant that the two formulae teach roughly the same thing, but argues that both ways of speaking are appropriate. Basil, however, does not find creedal formulae particularly helpful in themselves. One must understand them rightly. To help us with this, Basil offers a summary that shows us his own preferred language for saying how the Son is both one with the Father and distinct from him. It is more technical than the brief sentence we quoted earlier from *ep.* 9, but the point is roughly the same:

> But if someone takes the commonality of the substance to mean that one and the same formula of being is observed in both [Father and Son], such that if, hypothetically speaking, the Father is conceived of as light in his substrate, then the substance of the Only-Begotten is also confessed as light, and whatever one may assign to the Father as the formula of his being, the very same also applies to the Son. If someone takes the commonality of the substance in this way, we accept it and claim it as our doctrine. For this is how divinity is one. Clearly, their unity is conceived to be a matter of the formula of the substance. Hence while there is difference in number and in the distinctive features that characterize each, their unity is observed in the formula of the divinity.[9]

Later, it would be his preferred name for the three "persons."

7. *Eun.* 2.23

8. *Eun.* 2.22.

9. *Eun.* 1.19.

Basil's language requires some unpacking. For Eunomius, there is no "commonality of substance" between the Unbegotten and the Only-Begotten. In claiming that there is a sharing of substance, Basil has to state carefully in exactly what sense he means this. Perhaps the most obvious sense he wants to avoid is that of substance as material "stuff" possessed by both Father and Son. He also wants to qualify the language of "Father" and "Son." While Basil argues that these titles are literally true, they do not carry any connotations of physical reproduction. The Father's substance is not passed to the Son in the same way that genetic reproduction works. Nonetheless, the language of "Father" and "Son" does tell us that the two are of the same nature and that the Father is the cause of the Son. Fathers do not produce offspring that are different from them in nature.

So what does "commonality of substance" mean? It means that whatever title is applied to the Father by way of substance is also applied to the Son by way of substance. Basil calls this, alternatively, the "formula of being," the "formula of the substance," and the "formula of the divinity." If "light" is the Father's "formula of being," so too is it for the Son. This means that if you ask, "What is the Father?," the answer would be "light." And the same would apply to the Son. This is the sense in which Basil understands sharing of substance. What the Father is in his being is the same as what the Son is. Given our revealed language, we can say this much, even if we cannot perceive the divine light fully. But as soon as one affirms their commonality, one must account for how Father and Son are distinct from one another. Basil says they are distinct "in number and in the distinctive features which characterize each."

In *Against Eunomius*, Basil devotes a lot of energy to explaining what he means by "distinctive features" (*idiotētes*), which he also calls "distinguishing marks" (*idiōmata*). He draws an analogy with human names like "Peter" and "Paul." As humans, they share a common substance. But their proper names do not refer to this shared substance. Rather, these names communicate the individual's "distinctive features." "Peter" tells us that we are dealing with "the son of Jonah, the man from Bethsaida, the brother of Andrew, the one summoned from the fishermen to the ministry of the apostolate, the one who because of the superiority of his faith was charged with the building up of the church."[10] A similar list is invoked when we say "Paul." These names tell us the individual's unique character, not the properties shared with other humans in virtue of the shared human nature. The important point is that there is no contradiction between individuality and shared substance. Both are true. When it comes to the Father and the Son, the "distinguishing marks" simply are their fatherhood and sonship, respectively.[11] It is also true that the terms signify relation to the other: the Father is the unbegotten cause *of* the Son; the Son is the only-begotten Son *of* the Father. This does not undermine their equality in respect of those properties they share—light, life, power, and goodness. Just as all humans *qua* humans are equal, so too with the Father and the Son.

This does not mean that humans make a terribly good analogy for the Trinity. We do not. Basil did not offer a "social doctrine" of the Trinity, in which human community provides a paradigm for reflection on the Trinity. Such doctrines would become popular among theologians in

10. *Eun.* 2.4.

11. *Eun.* 2.28.

the twentieth century (despite what "human communities" were doing to each other then). The unity of Father and Son is infinitely greater than the unity of human nature and infinitely greater than even the finest human community's unity. By invoking two humans, Peter and Paul, on a merely logical level, Basil successfully shows us a case in which distinct individuals nonetheless share a commonality of substance. Another example he mentions is the set of specific differences for the genus "animal": we characterize species of animals as either footed or winged (in terms of their primary mode of movement), as aquatic or terrestrial, as rational or irrational.[12] Humans are footed, terrestrial, rational animals, whereas pigeons are winged, terrestrial, irrational animals. Neither species is any more or any less "animal" than the other. We could call this the "rule of unity-and-difference": one must not confuse shared properties (in this case, the properties that go with being an animal

12. It is not that the divide between rational and irrational is absolute in terms of actual behavior. Humans frequently forsake their true nature and instead act like beasts. And some animals can engage in at least elementary forms of reasoning. In his work *On the Six Days of Creation*, Basil notes that, when hunting, dogs perform basic syllogistic reasoning: "The dog is without reason but, nevertheless, he has sense reactions equivalent to reason. In fact, the dog appears to have been taught by nature what the wise of the world, who occupy themselves during life with much study, have solved with difficulty, I mean the complexities of inference. In tracking down a wild beast, if he finds the tracks separated in many directions, he traverses the paths leading each way and all but utters the syllogistic statement through his actions: 'Either the wild beast went this way,' he says, 'or this, or in that direction; but, since it is neither here nor there, it remains that he set out in that direction.' Thus, by the elimination of the false he finds the true way. What more do those do who settle down solemnly to their theories, draw lines in the dust, and then reject two of the three premises, finding the true way in the one that is left?" (Basil, *hom.* 9, *On the Six Days of Creation*; Way, 142–43). The idea is Stoic in origin.

regardless of what kind of animal you are) with distinctive features (those properties which make this species unique). The rule applies equally to the differences and similarities between Father and Son.

But the rule, valid as it is, does not carry us terribly far in understanding the Father and the Son. Like any purely logical rule, it does not by itself form the *content* of theological reflection.[13] It might help us to solve some problems. For instance, with the rule of unity-and-difference in mind, let us consider one of Eunomius's favorite verses, 1 Timothy 6:16, where God is said to "dwell in unapproachable light." The problem is how to interpret this *together* with something like John 1:9, where it is the Word of God who is called the "true light." For Eunomius, one of these "lights" differs from the other by as much as Unbegotten differs from Only-Begotten. For Basil, Eunomius conflates two different sets of properties: one set is shared between Father and Son, whereas the other distinguishes them.

But, again, it is crucial that we not carry these logical distinctions—perfectly valid though they are—too far. We must go past these rather abstract reflections on genera and species. After all, the various species of the genus animal are separable in our thinking. We can say quite a lot about humans without mentioning pigeons, and vice versa. And there are pairs of species—jellyfish and zebras, for instance—that obviously cannot live in the same habitat. This is not true of the Father and the Son. Basil's argument in *Against Eunomius* is not simply that the Son is "equal" to

13. As an example of Trinitarian reflection that is more to the point, I would cite (as one among many examples) *Eun.* 2.25, where Basil says that it is a basic datum of Christianity "that the Son is the begotten light who has shone forth from the unbegotten light, that he is life itself and goodness itself that has proceeded from the lifegiving source and the paternal goodness."

the Father in light, life, and so forth—though he does dwell on that point in order to counter Eunomius's claim about the Father's utter "incomparability." Zebras and jellyfish are equally animals. More fundamentally than the claim about the Son's equality, Basil wants us to see that the Son is *inseparable from the Father* in every way.

If the Son is entirely inseparable from the Father, then there never was a time when the Son did not exist. Yes, the Son was begotten, but the Logos was also with God "in the beginning," which for Basil means that there was no beginning for the Son's being.[14] The Son depends upon the Father for his being; the Father is the cause of the Son; Basil agrees that the Father is indeed "greater," as in John 14:28, in the sense of being the cause and principle of the Son's being.[15] But this is timeless causal dependence. One image Basil uses to help us think about this is the language from Hebrews of the Christ as the "radiance" of God's "glory" (Heb 1:3); God's glory being eternal, so too must be its radiance.[16] This argument is adapted from Origen and the tradition that he inspired of reflection upon paradigmatic scriptural passages.[17] When we reflect upon any of these re-

14. To drive this point home, Basil pairs John 1:1 with Ps 109:3: "From the womb before the daybreak I have begotten you" (*Eun.* 2.17).

15. See Basil's comments in *Eun.* 1.22–26, esp. 1.25.

16. *Eun.* 2.17.

17. See above, pp. 33–34. Basil says he is discussing *hupodeigmata* (examples), one of the Greek equivalents of *exempla*, at the beginning of *Eun.* 2.17, the section in which he invokes Heb 1:3, as well as the language of Christ as "image" (Col 1:15), "wisdom" and "power" (1 Cor 1:24) and "righteousness" (1 Cor 1:30). Of course, when it comes to interpreting such passages, there are important doctrinal similarities and differences between Origen and Basil: for instance, unlike Origen, Basil thought that creation is not eternal; like Origen, Basil believed God is eternally Father of the Son.

vealed *exempla*, we must do so in a way that imports none of the conditions of our created reality, including time, into the divine realm. The creation of the world is the creation of time. Outside of the created order, and in particular outside of the realm of *motion*, no temporal intervals can exist. So, it is absurd to speak of a "gap" which is "before" the Son. Terms like "before" and "after" make no sense where there is no time. So, Eunomius's attempt to separate the Son from God on the grounds that the Son is caused while God is uncaused (unbegotten) fails. Even Eunomius's assumption that the One Who Is in Exodus 3:14 is the Unbegotten God is false; following venerable patristic tradition, Basil argues that the burning bush scene during which this name is revealed is a manifestation (or theophany) of the divine Son before his incarnation.[18]

Another implication of the Son's inseparability from God has to do with the Son's role as revealer. Fundamental to Christianity is the claim that knowledge of God comes through the Son, who appeared in human form in Jesus Christ. If the two are entirely incomparable, Basil asks, how could the Son make the Father known to us? More precisely, how could it be the case that, in Jesus' words, "The one who sees me sees the one who sent me" (John 12:45)?[19] Christ himself, Basil says, is the "way upward to knowledge" of God.[20] In ordinary life, the way to some place need not be like that place in order to get us there; the road's utility in getting us to the destination is all that matters. But the case of knowing God is different. To be

18. *Eun.* 2.18. The identification of the speaker with Christ is confirmed by the observation that the speaker in the burning bush episode is alternatively called "the angel of the Lord" and "God."

19. Cited by Basil in *Eun.* 1.17.

20. *Eun.* 1.18.

sure, all humans can know something of God from looking at the world around them, perceiving God in its beauty and order. Or they can see God within themselves, as the ultimate source and object of their loves and interests. But this is reflected vision, as if in a mirror; seeing God *in* something that is not God. The Christian tradition insists on something deeper than this: "In your light we shall see light" (Ps 35:10 (LXX)/36:9). Here, the object of the vision and the medium through which we see are the same. The means and object are the divine light—for Basil, a shared attribute of the divine substance. In Christ, the mediator, who is light, we see the light that is God. Put in a simple analogy, "what perceptible light is to the eye, God the Word is to the soul."[21] For Basil, this is the meaning of the New Testament language of Christ as the "image" of God (e.g., 2 Cor 4:4; Col 1:15).[22] Since Christ is the one who enables our knowledge, to posit a God who is far beyond Christ, as Eunomius does, is to posit a God we could never know.[23] The "knowledge" of God that Christ does in fact bring is not of the sort that a purely human teacher or a created angel can impart.[24] The revealer and what is revealed are the same.

We must, then, understand the language of Christ as "light" and "image" properly. "Light" teaches us the equality of Christ with the Father. "Image" teaches us that Christ is the unique revealer of this light to us, and not merely as a painting represents something other than itself, but as himself the light which he conveys. So, Christ's

21. *Eun*. 2.16.

22. See *Eun*. 2.16–17.

23. *Eun*. 2.15.

24. Still, there is a tension here, since Basil retains the language of "angel" for Christ; see *Eun*. 2.18.

teaching—which Eunomius also emphasized—does not lead us to glorify the Father alone; Christ himself is shown to be inseparable from the Father's glory.

Now, of course, it is the *incarnate* Lord who reveals. Basil and Eunomius differ on how to understand the relation of Christ's humanity and divinity. While Eunomius insists upon the unity of Christ, Basil posits a distinction. Take a verse like Acts 2:36: "God made him both Christ and Lord, this Jesus whom you crucified." For Eunomius, this tells us that the Son is made by God, not merely in his humanity, but in an act of creation before the creation of the world. The Son's "divinity" is created. For Basil, the Son is eternally begotten, and not created. This passage refers to the Son's humanity. For Basil, there are two ways that scripture speaks about the Son: in the mode of "theology," or in reference to the "economy."[25] Passages of the former kind tell us about the eternal being of the Son; the latter refer to the incarnation. "In the beginning was the Word"—that's the language of theology. "Jesus grew in wisdom and stature"—that's the economy. If a passage tells us that Jesus grows up, that he is sent by God, that he obeys, or that he weeps, this passage is meant to tell us about his loving condescension to our level, his sharing in our reality. If a passage tells us about the Word's eternal being, this tells us of the Son's sharing in God's reality. We *distinguish* theology and economy, but never *separate* them. Because the two are closely connected, we cannot take the economic passages as indicating that the Son is inferior to the Father. Christ is not a servant by nature, ever the Father's "obedient Son," as Eunomius proclaimed.[26] He is the eternal Word of God, who remained "in the form of God," even as he freely and

25. *Eun.* 2.3; 2.15.

26. *Apol.* 27.

for our sakes emptied himself and took on the "form of a slave" (Phil 2:6).

The christological debate between Basil and Eunomius was about how we know God, and in particular about Christ's role as teacher and revealer. Basil and Eunomius interpreted this teaching quite differently. Eunomius believed that Christ taught us strictly to worship his Father and God as the Unbegotten One. His revelatory power is so strong that we can be sure that he has taught us the very essence of God. For Basil, this is to commit the basic error of claiming to know more than we can. While it might surprise those who think of doctrinal debate as principally a matter of trying to define God, a considerable amount of *Against Eunomius* is devoted to the incomprehensibility of God. In particular, Basil makes three points about Eunomius's favorite title for God, "Unbegotten": (1) it is a term of human invention or "conceptualization" (*epinoia*)—and is no less valid for that; (2) it is merely negative—it tells us what God is *not*, rather than what God is; and (3) it tells us *how* God is—that God does not come from any prior cause or source—rather than *what* God is. I have discussed these arguments at length elsewhere.[27] For now, it is worth noting how thoroughly Basil sets himself against any doctrine that attempts to tell us exactly and definitively what or who God is. While we have revealed language for God—the divine light, life, power, and so forth—these terms must not be taken as "dictionary definitions" of God, which one can master without a corresponding spiritual growth. Knowledge of God always involves participation in the divine light. This occurs only in and through Christ, who himself is the "power of God" (1 Cor 2:4), the "true light" (John 1:9; 8:12; etc.), and the "life" (John 14:6) we are called to share.

27. Radde-Gallwitz, *Basil, Gregory*, 122–42.

For Basil, Christ illumines the world with the divine light which he himself is by nature. Christ is equal in nature with the Father, whom he reveals to humanity. For Basil, in order for Christ to be a faithful image, he must *be* that which he makes manifest to us. In our weakness, we grasp this revelation through a myriad of names and titles, revealed to us mercifully by the one who emptied himself, taking on the form a slave and dwelling among us.

FOUR

Against Eunomius 3 and the Beginning of Debate over the Spirit

Every day, at the third hour (9:00 am), monks in the monasteries that Basil oversaw paused from their work and assembled for a service of prayer that especially commemorated the descent of the Holy Spirit upon the disciples at Pentecost.[1] Their prayer to the Spirit was to follow the Psalms, which they would have sung antiphonally at their

1. The association with Pentecost goes back at least to the early third century. It appears in two works from third-century Carthage: Tertullian, *On the Prayer* 25; and Cyprian, *On the Lord's Prayer* 34. It is also endorsed by John Cassian, who reports monastic practices in Palestine and Egypt (in *Institutes* 3, written in the 420s). Perhaps Basil learned this tradition in his tour of these locations. Given Cyprian's correspondence with Firmilian, the third-century bishop of Caesarea, the flow of ideas between Carthage and Cappadocia is not out of the question. For a different third-hour tradition, see Pseudo-Hippolytus, *Apostolic Tradition* 41.5–6 (Bradshaw et al., 196–97, and commentary on 207–8).

prayer services[2]: "Create a pure heart in me, O God, and renew an upright Spirit within me. Do not thrust me away from your presence and do not take away from me your Holy Spirit. Restore to me the joy of your salvation and strengthen me by your ruling Spirit" (Ps 50:12–13 LXX) and "May your Good Spirit guide me on level ground" (Ps 142:10 LXX).[3] These titles of the Spirit—upright, holy, ruling, and good—were not simply pious glosses. In Basil's mind, they teach us something of the Spirit's divine nature.

The final decades of the fourth-century Trinitarian controversies witnessed increasing attention to the question of the Holy Spirit. In the Nicene Creed, the Spirit received the briefest mention: "And [we believe] in the Holy Spirit." *What* one was to believe was left unsaid. In 381, the Council of Constantinople added, "the Lord, the giver of life, who proceeds from the Father; with the Father and the Son he is worshipped and glorified; He has spoken through the prophets." Basil died before this formula was crafted. There is no reason to believe that its crafters were influenced by Basil, or by his brother Gregory, who was at the council. Constantinople's additions regarding the Spirit perhaps would have pleased Basil. The creed's description of the Spirit as Giver of life and as worshipped and glorified with the Father and the Son echoes Basil's pneumatological (from *pneuma*, "Spirit," and *logos*, "rational account or doctrine") writings. However, we must not judge Basil's writings by later standards. We must remember that he was working out a doctrine to some extent on his own, with no council to confirm it and with fierce opposition from many, including friends.

2. See Basil, *ep.* 207 for his defense of this practice.

3. *LR* 37 (Holmes, 226), altered here for consistency.

Throughout his ecclesiastical career, Basil devoted considerable energy to discussing the Holy Spirit. His work *On the Holy Spirit* (374/75) is rightly considered one of the classic treatments of the subject. In this chapter, we begin our survey of Basil's writings on the Spirit, a project that will take us three chapters to complete. Here, we begin with the third book of *Against Eunomius*. Given the controversial nature of the topic in Basil's day, and the lack of clear answers in existing Christian literature, it is perhaps surprising that much of Basil's approach to pneumatology had already been worked out when he wrote this book. Many people saw his glorification of the Spirit's divinity as a problematic innovation, which would carry us far beyond the letter of Scripture, as traditionally interpreted.

But all this raises the question: *how* does one go about supporting—or opposing, for that matter—the divinity of the Spirit? Compared to Christ, the Spirit somehow seems more nebulous. While there is a host of biblical texts on the Spirit, there are problems with interpreting these. For instance, how do we know that the Spirit is not simply a messenger from God, an angel, an intermediate being between God and humans? After all, Scripture speaks of these as "ministering *spirits*" (Heb 1:14). It is true that, like Christ, the Spirit is spoken of as "sent" from God (Gal 4:4–6; John 14:26, etc.). But so too are the ministering spirits. Indeed, even John the Baptist was "sent from God" (John 1:6). Surely he was not divine. Perhaps the notion of the Spirit as an angel strikes us as peculiar, but we must bracket our inherited preconceptions and remember that the Spirit had been closely associated with angels in the Scriptures and in widely read early Christian documents like *The Shepherd of*

Hermas.[4] Let us turn to *Against Eunomius* to see how Basil defended the Holy Spirit's divinity.

Basil's Pneumatology in *Against Eunomius*

In his *Apology*, Eunomius expressed his view of the Spirit in terms of the categories of nature, activity, and dignity. This is important to note, since these are the very categories Basil himself would adopt: the Spirit's nature (who or what is the Spirit?; what have we learned from scripture to *call* the Spirit and what do these names teach us?); the Spirit's activities (what does the Spirit do?); and the Spirit's dignity (is the Spirit to be "ranked" *with* the Father and Son in worship?). Although Eunomius and Basil used classifications like these, both wanted to stick to the letter of Scripture. For both of them, Christ's baptismal formula in Matthew 28:19 is important. But they drew very different conclusions from it. For Basil, it proves the inseparability of the Father, Son, and Spirit. But Eunomius reasoned differently. He noted that the Spirit is placed third in the baptismal formula of Matthew 28:19, which for him signaled that the Spirit is third in rank or dignity. From this, he drew the conclusion that the Spirit's nature is third after the Father's and the Son's. For Eunomius, the order of the three must be preserved. It reveals, in descending degree, their dignity and nature. But he also spoke about the Spirit's activities. In keeping with broad biblical and patristic tradition, Eunomius affirms that the Spirit is "filled with the power of sanctification and instruction." Sanctifying the faithful and teaching them—these activities are unique to the Spirit.[5] But, crucially, the Spirit is "bereft of divinity

4. See Bucur, *Angelomorphic Pneumatology*.

5. See also Eunomius's *Confession of Faith* 4 (Vaggione, 157–59), which lists the activities of the Spirit, the "teacher of godliness": "he

and creative power."[6] The Spirit is never called, and thus is not Creator. The Spirit, or "Paraclete," is brought into being at God's command through the Only-Begotten Son. God "uses the Paraclete as a servant" for the activities of assuring, instructing, and sanctifying believers.[7] Eunomius's list of the Spirit's activities has precedent in Origen. In *On First Principles*, Origen famously states that all existing things participate in God, while only rational beings participate in the Word, and only the saints participate in the Spirit. That is, the scope of the Spirit's action is restricted to the faithful. Certainly, much of the biblical material on the Spirit has to do with instructing, guiding, and empowering God's people. One of the major questions of the debate about the Spirit is whether the Spirit is involved with all of God's actions (including those such as creation which have a far wider scope) or only with the lives of Christians.

Basil responded by arguing that Eunomius's use of Scripture is both overly restrictive and confused. Basil provided a much more extensive catalogue of passages on the Spirit. He divides his discussion of these in *Eun.* 3.2–4 into two parts: the first on the Spirit's nature, and the second on its activities.[8]

---

sanctifies the saints, initiates those approaching the Mystery, distributes every gift at the command of the Giver of grace, assists those who believe in the apprehension and contemplation of what has been commanded, inspires those who pray, leads us to that which is advantageous, strengthens us in godliness, enlightens souls with the light of knowledge, cleanses our thoughts, binds demons and heals the sick, cures the diseased, raises the fallen, refreshes the weary, encourages the struggling, cheers the fainthearted . . ."

6. *Apol.* 25.

7. *Apol.* 27.

8. These come in 3.2–3 and 3.4, respectively. In 3.7, Basil takes up the disputed verses John 1:3 and Amos 4:13. His discussion of those verses is dependent upon Didymus the Blind's work *On the Holy*

It is illogical, Basil reasons, to infer from the Spirit's third place in the baptismal formula that it is third in nature. When the Spirit appears together with God and Christ, it is not always listed third. More importantly, Basil cites many passages that, in his mind, reveal the "magnificence of the nature of the Holy Spirit."[9] His treatment of these verses is based upon a fundamental division:

> It is said that there are two realities: divinity and creation, sovereignty and servitude, sanctifying power and sanctified power, that which has virtue by nature and that which achieves virtue by freewill. In which class shall we rank the Spirit? Among those who are sanctified? But it is sanctity itself. Perhaps among those who come to possess virtue by good deeds? But it is good by nature.[10]

Basil distinguishes between those things that have a property, such as goodness, by participation, and that which is good by nature, simply in virtue of being what it is. When we look at biblical passages on the Spirit's nature, we must bear this dichotomy in mind. To explain it, Basil uses his beloved example of iron heated in fire. Here, the point of the analogy is to stress that fire has heat as a natural property, whereas iron does not. While it is true that both the heated iron and the fire are hot, fire is so by its very nature, whereas iron is so only by its contact with fire. Similarly, both God and an angel are holy. However, God is so by nature, whereas the angel (or a saintly person) is so derivatively. Just as iron can be iron while changing from cool to

---

Spirit, which was written between Eunomius's *Apology* in 360 and Basil's *Eun.* in 364/65. See DelCogliano, "Basil, Didymus, and Exegesis."

9. *Eun.* 3.4.

10. *Eun.* 3.2 (DelCogliano and Radde-Gallwitz [FotC 122], 187-88), altered for consistency.

hot and back, so too can an angel become holy and lose holiness. But God can no more be unholy than fire can be cold. This is what we mean when we say that holiness is the nature of God. And Basil has already shown in the first two books *Against Eunomius* that titles attributed to the Father's nature are shared with the Son. So, both Father and Son are holy by nature. But, "holy" is of course especially ascribed to the Spirit in Scripture, so much so that we can confidently claim that "holiness is the Spirit's nature."[11] This means that the Spirit, along with Father and Son, is the source of holiness for created beings, not in the way that heated iron could in turn heat other objects, but as the fire that heats of its own nature. If the question is, "What or who is the Spirit?," the best answer is, "Sanctity itself."

What goes for holiness also goes for other terms associated with the Spirit in Scripture: "goodness" (the Spirit is called "good Spirit" in Ps 142:10 LXX) and "Paraclete." As the Spirit is holy by nature, so too is the Spirit by nature good. And the fact that the Son also is called "Paraclete" (for instance, in John 14:16) shows that the Spirit shares the Son's nature.

Basil makes two assumptions worth noting. First, the revealed language of Scripture is the primary guide for theological reflection. The names of the Spirit tell us something about who the Spirit is by nature. Of course, the Spirit's nature remains incomprehensible, and revealed language employs metaphor and enigma. We can know *that* the Spirit is holiness, but saying exactly *what* holiness is eludes us. Yet, it is worth noting the emphasis he placed upon the titles of the Spirit in the bible as guides to reflection and inquiry. Second, the divine/created distinction is absolute, and Basil engages in a disciplined attempt to

11. *Eun.* 3.3; also said in 3.2.

keep it so. Of course, Eunomius also sought to keep the Unbegotten God distinct from all else—though Eunomius appeared to Basil to be quite fuzzy regarding the status of the Son, who is, according to Eunomius, not God in the way the Unbegotten is, but is nonetheless *our* Lord and God. The problem of distinguishing God from the world was in fact more difficult for Basil than for Eunomius. As long as one focuses exclusively on the title "Unbegotten," it is easy to show the difference. We are all decidedly begotten; all created things come into being and pass away. But Basil focuses on a much wider range of divine names. His list includes terms that are applied both to God and to creatures, such as the adjective "good." This forces Basil to elaborate upon the difference between inherent or natural goodness—which the Father, Son, and Spirit alone possess—and the goodness we see around us in our ordinary lives. When things or people can be thought of as good or desirable, this is not what makes them what they are, as it is for God (though one has to drop the phrase "makes them" in the case of God). When we say, "God is good," we do not mean that God is like a lot of other things that can also be called good. We mean that God *is* goodness. This is not true of a good coat or a good friend (we can think of coats that are not desirable and of false friends). So for Basil, the task of distinguishing God from the world is the same as the task of distinguishing pure goodness from limited and derivative examples of it. The latter are not to be spurned or looked down upon; indeed, Basil's argument implies that we are to look at the goodness and beauty within them as manifestations of God's goodness and beauty; they are, nonetheless, not to be confused with God. We are to see them as signs pointing beyond themselves to the one who is and cannot be other than goodness itself. God is the goodness behind every genuinely good thing we desire in life, and the life at the center of all life.[12] As the "good Spirit," the same goes for the Holy Spirit. Inseparable from the Father and the Son, the Spirit is the fount of every good thing. This is Basil's understanding of the Spirit's nature in *Against Eunomius*; we will see it again in later works.

As for the Spirit's activities, Basil lists several. The Spirit is involved in the act of creation, but in a unique manner. Interestingly, Basil stops short of calling the Spirit "Creator." He notes the difference between the activities of the Word and those of the Spirit in Psalm 32:6 (LXX): "By the Word of the Lord the heavens were made firm, and by the Spirit of his mouth all their power." Basil takes "power" here as a reference to the "heavenly powers," that is, what we typically generically call "angels." While the heavens are created by the Word, those who occupy the heavens are made firm and steadfast by the Spirit. This is an important point. While Basil does not affirm here that the Spirit is Creator, he does make a crucial move for the debate at hand when he stresses that the Spirit sanctifies and confirms the heavenly powers.[13] If the Spirit sanctifies the heavenly powers, then the Spirit is not one of them.

The Spirit also sanctifies humans. Citing Job 33:4, Basil argues that humans are made perfect in virtue by the Spirit. This is not all that different from Eunomius or Origen. Like them, Basil speaks of the Spirit as teacher of the faithful. However, Basil differs in that he makes the Spirit's work inseparable from Christ's own work of instruction, a point he makes by juxtaposing Matthew 23:9–10 with

12. *LR* 2.

13. This point remains central throughout Basil's career: see, e.g., *Spir.* 16.38. There Basil makes clear that the Spirit's role of "confirming" the heavenly powers means "making them perfect in holiness."

John 14:26. Similarly, the adoption of Christians as "sons of God" occurs both through Christ (John 1:12) and the Spirit (Rom 8:15). By citing passages that attribute the same action to both Christ and the Spirit, Basil supports his basic thesis of the Spirit's inseparability from God and God's Son.

Basil focuses on four additional biblical passages that expand the picture of the Spirit's activities. First, there is 1 Corinthians 12:4–6, 11. Basil notes the parallelism among the phrases "same Spirit," "same Lord," and "same God" in these verses and concludes that Paul is making a point about their shared activities. He also reasons that if the Spirit is said to act "as it wills" (1 Cor 12:11) then the Spirit is not a mere servant of God and Christ, as Eunomius thought. Rather, it has "nothing other than authoritative and sovereign power." The Spirit's agency shows its equality in power with the Father and the Son.[14]

The second passage also comes from 1 Corinthians (2:11–12): "No one knows the things that belong to a human being except the human spirit that is in him; likewise, no one knows the things that belong to God except the Spirit of God." If the Spirit is to God as the soul is to its own "internal reasonings," then the Spirit cannot be thought of as "strange" or "foreign" to God.[15]

Third, Basil cites Romans 8:11: "The one who raised Christ Jesus from the dead will also give life to our mortal bodies through his Spirit who dwells in you." Now, God is the one who "gives life to all things" (1 Tim 6:13), and Christ as shepherd gives "everlasting life" to his sheep (John 10:27–28). When we take these verses together, we see the Trinitarian structure of the divine activity of

14. *Eun.* 3.4.

15. *Eun.* 3.4.

the resurrection of the body: "God lavishes life upon us through Christ in the Holy Spirit."[16]

Fourth, Basil moves to the mystery of divine indwelling in us. Eunomius wrote that the Spirit is "bereft of divinity and creative power." Basil responds in an interesting manner: "He who says this seems not to believe that the divinity is in us." That is, Eunomius is not simply denying some "fact" about the Holy Spirit as an objective reality. He is saying something about God's presence within us. Basil cites three passages that claim that God dwells in us through the Spirit.[17] If it is "in the Spirit" that we are made into a "habitation *of God*" (Eph 2:21–22), then the Spirit must be divine. Basil then alludes to the practice of speaking of salvation as "deification," being made divine: "And if we call those who are perfect in virtue 'gods,' and this perfection comes through the Spirit, how does it make others gods if it is itself bereft of divinity?"[18]

Basil shows that the actions of the Spirit mentioned in the Scriptures are more varied than Eunomius held them to be. If Spirit acts in all these ways, it must be inseparably linked by nature with God. It is incoherent to attribute these actions to it if it is merely a created servant of God like an angel. An angel can announce God's wishes to humanity, but does so at God's command rather than "as it wishes" (1 Cor 12:11). An angel can incite humans to do good deeds, but cannot dwell in us, making us the temple of God. These actions show us the nature of the Spirit. As for the Spirit's dignity, Basil surprisingly concedes Eunomius's point that the Spirit is third in "rank and dignity."[19] What this means

16. *Eun.* 3.4.

17. 1 John 3:24; 1 Cor 3:16; and Eph 2:21–22.

18. *Eun.* 3.5.

19. *Eun.* 3.1.

is rather unclear: is the Spirit not honored along with the Father and the Son? Later in his career, Basil will insist that the Spirit shares the divine dignity. But in *Against Eunomius*, Basil lacks the clarity we assume from the standpoint of later orthodoxy. He is adamant that the Spirit shares the divine nature, and that the Spirit's activities show this. The divine dignity is a separate matter for him at this point.

There is another point where Basil is less than clear. Whereas most of *Eun.* 3 is a straightforward response to Eunomius's own words, in a final section Basil brings up a viewpoint that we have no evidence of Eunomius holding. Basil argues against an unnamed "they" who use John 1:3 together with Amos 4:13 to argue that the Spirit is a creature.[20] This argument is not made in Eunomius's *Apology*. It is addressed in another work from the period, Didymus the Blind's *On the Holy Spirit*. Didymus does not tell us against whom he is arguing; it is merely one argument among many that Didymus addresses in his defense of the Spirit's divinity. But it was clearly made by some group active in the early 360s. Basil is subtly associating Eunomius with this broader group and attributing their arguments to him. While this might appear disingenuous, it is in fact likely that there were actual connections between Eunomius and the group Didymus attacks. At any rate, it is worth noting that as early as 364/65 Basil is aware of a broader current of debate on the Spirit than simply what he finds written in Eunomius. His subsequent works on the Spirit will address such a group, though often with the categories and methods he had already developed by the time he wrote *Eun.* 3. With the categories of nature, activity, and dignity in hand, Basil could scour the language of Scripture and tradition for exemplary notions of the Spirit.

20. *Eun.* 3.7.

FIVE

Basil's Career: From *Against Eunomius* to *On the Holy Spirit*

The roughly ten years between *Against Eunomius* and Basil's major work, *On the Holy Spirit*, were momentous for Basil. He wrote the former during his third ascetic retreat in Annisa. In 365, Basil returned to Caesarea and again assumed pastoral duties under the metropolitan bishop Eusebius. The two had had a falling out, and it took sensitive letters by Gregory of Nazianzus to mediate their reconciliation. Gregory understood that the rather inept Eusebius would require Basil's theological talents in offering a defense against the Homoians, who were once again in favor under Emperor Valens (364–78). Basil served under Eusebius for the next five years, until Eusebius's death in 370. During this time, Basil's talents were required in an unforeseen way.

A particularly dry winter in 369–70 caused the grain crop to fail, and famine struck Cappadocia.[1] Basil was still dealing with its effects in 372, two years into his episcopacy. Eusebius, who lived through September 370, entrusted Basil with the organization of relief efforts in Caesarea. Basil endeavored (apparently successfully) to convince wealthy citizens who controlled the grain storehouses to sell surplus to him so that he could distribute it to the hungry, many of whom had been dislocated from Caesarea's rural hinterland because of the famine. He preached a series of sermons as part of his campaign of "shaming" the rich—who tend to be immune from the devastating effects of food shortage—into acting in the common interest. Famine, after all, is a result of political and moral failure—a failure of those who control the distribution of surplus to ensure that sufficient amounts are available at affordable prices—as much as of crop failure.[2] Gregory of Nyssa tells us that Basil depleted his own resources to provide food for the hungry at this time. He further specifies that Basil distributed to all equally, including "the children of the Jews."[3]

Basil's advocacy in this time of dire need no doubt won him support among the people of Caesarea. In 370, bishop Eusebius died. In order to understand the circumstances by

1. I have profited greatly from the excellent account in Holman, *The Hungry Are Dying*, esp. 64–134. Holman's book also includes her translation of Basil's *Homily* 8, *In Time of Famine and Drought* (183–92). For 370 as the year of the famine (as opposed to the customary date 368), see Lenski, *Failure of Empire*, 388–90.

2. For famine as a political problem, see Amartya Sen, quoted in Holman, *The Hungry Are Dying*, 66.

3. G. Nyssa, *Encomium on His Brother Basil* 17 (Stein, 39). One might wonder how Basil had resources after his renunciation. It is clear that he continued to receive an income from his family's estate: see Basil, *ep*. 37.

which Basil became his successor, we need a bit of context. At this time, bishoprics across the Roman Empire came in two kinds: metropolitan sees, which in most cases were located in the capital cities of Roman provinces, and sees throughout the province that were subordinate to the metropolitan. Also, a third category, the supermetropolitan, was emerging, which included major cities such as Alexandria, Antioch, and Rome, which had authority over broad regions. As capital of Cappadocia, Caesarea was a metropolis. According to customary practice and to the (often ignored) canons of Nicaea, in order to become bishop, one had to be both elected by the people and consecrated by the bishops of one's province. The metropolitan bishop was to oversee the process, though of course this was not possible when it was an election for the metropolitan office itself. Nonetheless, in any case, it was required that at least three bishops consecrate a bishop. The ideal was for there to be consensus among all the province's bishops in their choice. However, in cases where two or three bishops dissented from the majority opinion, the majority was to win the day. Moreover, there were strictures against bishops from other provinces meddling in the consecration.

Basil's consecration broke nearly all of these rules. The sequence of events leading up to it is somewhat obscure, but it seems to have gone as follows.[4] Basil was popular with the people of Caesarea, who apparently supported him as Eusebius's successor; while there is no record of an election favoring Basil, such would have been customary. However, there was a gathering of the province's bishops—perhaps thirteen in all—to discuss the matter. For unknown reasons, they were not on Basil's side. One Cappadocian bishop was not invited, and that was Basil's friend and mentor,

4. See the discussion in Norton, *Episcopal Elections*, 215–23.

Gregory the Elder, bishop of Nazianzus, the father of Basil's friend.[5] It was of course illicit for the Cappadocian bishops to exclude Gregory the Elder from this meeting.

Basil, still a presbyter in Caesarea, knew of this synod and contrived a rather deceptive, but effective scheme to influence events. He wrote a letter—now lost—to his friend Gregory saying that he was ill and indeed on his deathbed. In tears, Gregory hurried to say farewell to his longtime friend in the metropolis, only to discover Basil doing reasonably well. More importantly, he found the synod underway. He wrote a letter chastising Basil for his deviousness, realizing that Basil's intent had been to get Gregory to come to Caesarea. *Why* Basil wanted him there is less than clear. Neither Basil nor Gregory was yet a bishop, and thus neither had the right to consecrate a new bishop. But Basil knew that Gregory would be sure to inform his father about the meeting. Perhaps Basil was ambitious for the episcopal throne and wanted Gregory the Elder's support. Or perhaps he wanted his friend to be on the spot at the right time so that Gregory would be consecrated. Whatever Basil's motive, the effect was that his friend Gregory wrote three important letters in his father's name. Two were addressed to the bishops in Caesarea. In these, he offered his unequivocal support for the consecration of Basil.[6] The third was sent to (another) Eusebius, bishop of the city Samosata on the banks of the Euphrates River.[7] Gregory urged Eusebius to come and help supply

5. It is somewhat confusing that both Gregory the Elder and his (more famous) son are known as Gregory of Nazianzus. The son was never officially bishop of that city, though he did assist his elderly father in that capacity and took over administrative functions upon the latter's death in 374.

6. G. Naz., *epp.* 41, 43.

7. G. Naz., *ep.* 42.

Basil with the required number of consecrators. Eusebius's see did not lie in Cappadocia, which meant that he had no canonical right to grant Gregory's request. But grant it he did. Indeed, it was not the only time this "roving consecrator" engaged in such questionable activity in the interest of installing bishops sympathetic to Nicene Trinitarianism.[8] Together with the Gregory the Elder, who journeyed to the metropolis despite his ill health, Eusebius assured Basil's consecration. But because of Eusebius's role and because the will of the majority of Cappadocian bishops was overturned, Basil's elevation to the dignity of episcopal office was clouded with accusations of illegality. To avoid the appearance of simply being "Basil's man," his friend Gregory avoided visiting him for some time after his elevation, despite Basil's urgent requests for assistance in a chaotic time.[9] Despite the questions that Eusebius of Samosata's support must have raised, Basil never lapsed in his gratitude toward him.[10] By letter, he also seems to have received the support of Meletius of Antioch, despite the fact that the latter was in exile.[11] To be recognized as a bishop in communion with the church of Antioch would go a long way towards buoying Basil's cause.

Basil continued his efforts at poor relief. A short distance from Caesarea, he built a new complex which included a prayer house, a residence for the bishop and other clergy, a hostel for visitors, a hospital, and what he called a *ptōchotropheion*, a place for feeding the poor. Here, the

8. The phrase is Norton's description of Eusebius: *Episcopal Elections*, 164, 220.

9. G. Naz., *epp.* 45, 46.

10. Nineteen letters from Basil to Eusebius survive, all but one (*ep.* 27) from the period of Basil's episcopacy.

11. See Basil, *ep.* 57.

nourishment was not only physical: those in need could also be employed and receive training in various crafts.[12] It was a stunning accomplishment, and the "new city" began to be referred to as the "Basileias"—the city of Basil. It survived long after Basil's death.

We should remember that the staunchly anti-Nicene Valens was impressed with Basil's organization of famine relief. Despite their differences, Valens entrusted Basil with oversight of the churches in Armenia, particularly over the appointment of bishops.[13] Yet, Valens also made a move that threatened to curtail the extent of Basil's influence, though it likely was not intentionally directed against Basil: in 372, he divided Cappadocia into two provinces, the new one centered on Tyana. Anthimus, the new bishop there, believed Tyana to be a metropolis. To counter his influence, Basil set about installing sympathetic bishops into sees across his province, some of which he had to create anew. He made his brother Gregory bishop of Nyssa and his friend Gregory bishop of Sasima. Neither man took the appointment in good spirits. The blow was particularly hard for Nazianzen. Basil's younger brother, after all, could be expected to comply. But his longtime *friend*? The two never reconciled.[14] Although he allowed himself to be consecrated by Basil and his father, Gregory never took up administrative duties in Sasima. He spent some time in seclusion, pleading the cause of the philosophical life over against the public life of church politics. But he was

12. Basil describes the building of the complex in *ep.* 94. See also *ep.* 176, where he uses the term *ptōchotropheion*. See Holman, *The Hungry are Dying*, 74–76.

13. Basil's work in this area is detailed by Rousseau, *Basil of Caesarea*, 278–88.

14. See G. Naz., *or.* 43.59.

called by his aging father to Nazianzus, where the younger Gregory became the city's *de facto* Christian leader.

The Holy Spirit: Economy and Theology

Before turning to Basil's *On the Holy Spirit* in the next chapter, we should recount Basil's theology of the Spirit in works prior to that classic treatise, since it builds upon a prior foundation. In *ep.* 9, which we have already mentioned, Basil offers a brief, but instructive remark. The broader purpose of the letter is to discuss the theology of Dionysius, head of Alexandria's catechetical school and later bishop of Alexandria in the mid third century, a time of violent persecution of Christians and, predictably, internal debate among Christians. Dionysius was particularly opposed to Sabellius. Dionysius searched for a way to distinguish God the Father, and found it by claiming that "unbegottenness" is his essence. In Basil's view, it was a clear anticipation of Eunomius. Basil was not entirely unsympathetic towards Dionysius; it was, after all, his entirely justified zeal in combating Sabellius that led him too far in the opposite direction. He cites Dionysius's doxology with approval in *On the Holy Spirit*. He also commends Dionysius for using the language of "three hypostases" for the Father, Son and Spirit.[15] But Basil suggests that not only Dionysius's

15. *Spir.* 29.72. Basil himself first used "three hypostases" in *Eun.* 3.3. However, only in 376 did it become his preferred language for naming the three. See *epp.* 210, 236, 258. Like Dionysius, Basil used "hypostasis" to distinguish himself from Sabellius. He also was mapping his position on the schism in Antioch, where those who supported Meletius spoke of three hypostases, whereas the followers of Paulinus admitted only one divine hypostasis. The term was equivalent to *ousia* for the Paulinists. In Basil's own writings, despite his use of "three hypostases," there is a conflicting strand of thought that states that there can be no plurality, and hence no counting to three,

teaching on the Son, but also his views on the Spirit were problematic: Dionysius was guilty of "banishing the Spirit from the divinity we worship, and classifying it somewhere below, with the created and ministering nature."[16] In a sense, this is a passing remark that we can pass over quickly. Basil does not provide a theological argument that would specify *why* the Spirit is to be classified with the Father and the Son. Unlike *Against Eunomius*, there is no mention of the Spirit's nature. But the phrase reveals a great deal about Basil's teaching. Of central importance for Basil is the verb "classifying . . . with" (in Greek, the compound *syn-arithmein*—literally, "to count with"), which Basil also used in *Against Eunomius*, around the time of *ep.* 9.[17] Basil implies that the Spirit *is* to be worshipped with the divinity and that the Spirit *is not* to be classified with the creation, even with the ministering spirits who form the apex of the created order. Upon reading this, one knows immediately to draw the line between divinity and creation, and to place the Spirit on the divine side.

The language of the Spirit as "classified with" and "worshipped with" God occurs frequently in Basil's writings. He most famously defended these phrases in his *On the Holy Spirit* against those who would count the Spirit *below* (rather than *with*) the Father and the Son and would therefore find worship of the Spirit inappropriate. The same appears throughout Basil's correspondence as well. The following sentence, from *ep.* 52, is typical in its use of Matthew 28:19, which Basil takes as the statement of Christ's

---

when it comes to the monadic, singular divine nature. See *Eun.* 3.7 and *Spir.* 18.44–45; cf. below, p. 118, n. 23.

16. Basil, *ep.* 9.

17. *Eun.* 3.2 and 3.7.

own teaching on the matter, and hence the standard for ecclesiastical doctrine:

> The Holy Spirit is classified with the Father and Son, hence it also is above creation. We have learned its rank from the words of the Lord in the Gospel: *Go and baptize in the name of the Father, and of the Son, and of the Holy Spirit* (Mt 28:19).[18]

The Spirit's place along with Father and Son in the baptismal formula shows it is "above creation." Yet, its place after the Father and Son—in just that order—must be maintained. With this emphasis on the Trinitarian order, we see the continuing influence of the anti-Sabellian Homoiousian tradition on Basil; this sits alongside Basil's commitment to the full divinity of the Spirit. In the same letter, Basil does innovate on prior tradition in a phrase that is often misunderstood. Basil follows 1 Corinthians 2:12 in speaking of the Spirit as coming "from God." Basil expands the point: "Unless the Spirit is from God and is through Christ, it does not exist at all."[19] The baptismal order—Father, Son, Spirit—is important to maintain, not only because it reflects the risen Christ's commands regarding baptism, but also because it teaches us the origins of the Spirit. One cannot, therefore, place the Spirit before the Father or between the Father and the Son. He comes from God through Christ.

As bishop, Basil's teaching on the Spirit began to generate criticism from diametrically opposed sides. Around 372, Basil's relationship with his former mentor and friend Eustathius crumbled.[20] Recall that Basil was charged with

18. Basil, *ep.* 52.

19. Typically mistranslated, "If the Spirit is not from God, but is through Christ, it does not exist at all."

20. Unfortunately, we possess no writings from Eustathius.

overseeing the churches in Armenia, a task he shared with Theodotus, the bishop of Nicopolis. Like Basil, Theodotus was a supporter of Nicaea. But Theodotus was deeply suspicious of Eustathius, believing him to be heretical. For Theodotus, Basil was tainted by association. Basil sought to reconcile the two. After failing to get either of the two to produce a written statement of faith to present to the other, Basil took matters into his own hands. He would produce a statement of faith, have Eustathius sign it, and then present it to Theodotus, thereby assuring the latter of Eustathius's orthodoxy.

In 373, Basil drew up a statement. This document is preserved as his *ep.* 125. It contains an interesting account of Nicaea. Basil writes that, while this creed demands our assent, we must also see that its teaching on the Spirit is incomplete. This is not because the faith of the fathers was incomplete, but simply because the question had not been raised at that point. Basil also wants to be sure that Nicaea is not interpreted in a Sabellian direction. Additionally, the Spirit must be seen as "holy by nature," just as the Father and the Son are. This means that the Spirit is not sanctified, as the heavenly powers are, but sanctifies. One must not, therefore, remove the Spirit "from the divine and blessed nature." He lists a series of positions on the Spirit that are to be anathematized, including the view that the Spirit is one of the ministering spirits of Hebrews 1:14.[21] The efforts at reconciliation were unsuccessful. Eustathius signed Basil's creed, but soon renounced it. He continued

21. In *epp.* 113 and 114, Basil similarly recommends a minimum set of standards for reconciliation with Pneumatomachians: acceptance of the Nicene Creed and confession that the Spirit is not a creature. For discussion, see Haykin, "And Who Is the Spirit?"

to slander Basil.[22] He and his partisans began to accuse Basil of a number of errors, including innovation regarding the Spirit.[23] He sought to paint him as a Sabellian, a heretical tendency he believed had its roots in Basil's correspondence with Apollinarius as a young man. But to Basil, it was Eustathius who had changed his tune. Eustathius once railed against the Council of Constantinople, traveled to Rome and brought back the Nicene faith to Tyana. He had now abandoned the Nicene confession and joined with the very party put in power at Constantinople. Basil later spoke of this as a time of serious dejection, of a loss of faith in humankind.[24]

The other line of opposition to Basil's teaching on the Spirit also involved a former friend. Gregory of Nazianzus already had good personal reasons to be upset with Basil. Now doctrinal differences began to emerge. A certain monk had been present at a sermon Basil gave at the feast in memory of the local martyr St. Eupsychius on September 7, 372.[25] At a symposium shortly thereafter, at which Nazianzen was present, the same monk heard speeches praising Basil and Gregory. The monk sobered the mood: "Basil and Gregory are falsely praised; the former, because

22. For the context of *ep.* 125, see *epp.* 99, 130, 244.

23. See Basil, *ep.* 226.

24. *Ep.* 244 (D 3:459–61).

25. According to the fifth-century church historian Sozomen (*CH* 5.11), Eupsychius was a nobleman in Caesarea who participated in the destruction of a pagan Temple to Fortune. For this, he was martyred under the pagan revivalist Emperor Julian (361–63). Basil actively promoted his cult, celebrated annually on September 7. Basil would invite friends, notables, and bishops to the celebration, thus using the feast to cement his network. See Basil, *epp.* 100 (to Eusebius of Samosata), 142 (to the Governor's Accountant), 200 (to Amphilochius), and 252 (to the bishops of the civil diocese of Pontus).

his words are a betrayal of the faith, the latter, because his toleration aids the treason." Asked to elaborate, he explained that at the recent martyr festival, Basil spoke "most beautifully and perfectly upon the Godhead of the Father and the Son . . . but he slurred over the Spirit."[26] It has been suggested that the sermon he heard was the piece that has come down to us as *Homily* 15 and given the title *On the Faith*.[27] We cannot be certain that this is the sermon Basil preached on that occasion.[28] However, it does contain an account of the three Trinitarian persons, and a particularly rich section on the Spirit. It is therefore worthy of our attention. In fact, we can even see why, if the monk heard this sermon, he might have found it objectionable.

Basil begins with a sense of trepidation: although piety demands us to be constantly mindful of God, speaking about God is fraught with danger and difficulty. Still, casting our minds beyond the sensory realm to the true beauty, we find, beyond all heavenly powers: "There is Father, Son, and Holy Spirit—the uncreated nature, the dignity of the Lord, the natural goodness."[29] He proceeds to outline how we should think about the three:

> The Father is the first principle of all, the cause of being for those things which are, the root of living things. From him proceeds the source of life (cf. John

26. G. Naz., *ep.* 58, to Basil (*NPNF*[2] 7:455). For commentary, see McGuckin, *Saint Gregory of Nazianzus*, 216–18.

27. Jean Bernardi, *Prédication des Pères Cappadociens*, 85–86.

28. It is noteworthy that *Hom.* 15 has nothing to say about Eupsychius. However, this is no objection to its having been preached at his feast, since we do not know that such homilies always had the martyr as their subject. Moreover, it is on the Trinity, which corresponds well to what the anonymous monk reported to Nazianzen.

29. Basil, *Hom.* 15.2 (PG 31:465C); the point is repeated at *Hom.* 15.3 (PG 31:468C).

> 4:14); the *wisdom*, *power* (1 Cor 1:24), exact *image of the invisible God* (Col 1:15); the Son who was begotten from the Father; the living Word; he who is both *God* and *with God* (John 1:1); who does not come into being; who exists before the ages and is not acquired later; Son, not possession; Maker, not made; Creator, not creature; being everything that the Father is (cf. Jn 16:15, 17:10).

Basil cites several passages on the Son's eternal being and makes reference to the Nicene phrase "from the substance" (*ek tēs ousias*).[30] He touches upon the incarnate economy, which he stresses should not be used to diminish the Son's eternal glory.[31]

He then turns to the Spirit and offers an overview of the essentials regarding the Spirit's nature. If one could rise above created things in one's vision, one would see the Holy Spirit where the Father and Son are; the Spirit "also has by nature and essentially (*synousiōmenōs*) all things: goodness, righteousness, holiness, and life."[32] It is crucial

30. Basil, *Hom.* 15.2 (PG 31:468B). Here Basil qualifies the phrase thusly: the Son "shines forth from the substance with no gap [between them], being connected to the Father in a non-temporal manner, equal in goodness, equal in power, sharer of his glory." "From the substance" was part of the Nicene Creed of 325, but is not found in the Creed promulgated at Constantinople in 381; it is thus not part of the Creed recited by Christians today. Basil also cites "from the substance" in *Eun.* 2.23 (AD 364/65) and in three letters from 370–73, *epp.* 52, 125, and 140.

31. Basil says that when Christ made the following statements and others like them, he was speaking in reference to his bodily form: that he was sent (John 7:29, 8:42, 17:8, etc.), that he can do nothing on his own (5:19), and that he received a command (12:49).

32. Basil, *Hom.* 15.3 (PG 468C–D). In support, Basil cites Ps 142:10 (LXX); Ps 50:12, 13; Rom 8:2. In the quoted passage, *sunousiōmenōs* does not mean "consubstantially with the Father and the Son" but something like "bound up with the Spirit's own being,"

that one understand the attributes rightly. Basil stresses two points:

1. The Spirit possesses these attributes by nature. These attributes are therefore inseparable from the Spirit, just as heat is inseparable from fire.
2. The Spirit's natural attributes are no more depleted when they are given to creatures than the sun is depleted by shining on many different places at once.[33] Basil uses the language of "participation" to describe how creatures share in, but do not exhaust, the Spirit.[34]

After describing the Spirit's role in the rebirth of the apostles, Basil ends with a rhetorical flourish that opens new perspectives on the Spirit's role in the economy of salvation:

> This Spirit remains in heaven and fills the earth. It is present everywhere and is contained nowhere. It dwells entirely in each place and is wholly with God. It does not administer its blessings as a servant, but distributes the gifts with authority. For *the Spirit distributes to each one individually just as the Spirit wishes* (1 Cor 12:11). It *is sent* (Jn 14:26, 15:26, 16:7) as part of the economy, but it *acts* (1 Cor 12:11) on its own authority.[35]

as it does in *ep.* 159.

33. One must recall, of course, that like all ancients, Basil did not think of the sun as having a limited lifespan. Barring a cataclysmic event, it will keep on orbiting, illuminating, and warming the earth. Understood in this way, the sun provides a good analogy for the inexhaustibility of the Spirit.

34. The close pairing of participation language with talk of the Spirit "filling" creatures (here, angels and archangels) suggests the influence of Didymus's *On the Holy Spirit* on Basil.

35. Basil, *Hom.* 15.3 (PG 31:472A).

In this brief section, Basil makes three remarkable moves. First, he shows the importance of certain "philosophical" concepts for understanding Christian doctrine. He invokes the closely related ideas of divine simplicity, undiminished giving, and the integral omnipresence of being.[36] Divine simplicity is the idea that God is not divisible into parts. According to the idea of undiminished giving, God gives of himself without any loss or depletion on God's part. The notion of undiminished giving was perhaps most concisely stated in antiquity in the Wisdom of Solomon, where it is said of divine Wisdom that, "while remaining in herself, she renews all things" (Wis 7:27).[37] The idea appears frequently in Platonist writings from the Roman period. It had long been appropriated by Jewish authors such as Philo of Alexandria and Christians such as Origen and Didymus. The idea of undiminished giving marks a contrast between immaterial reality—believed to be more fully real and alive—and the material realm of becoming. Material things and possessions obviously cannot be distributed without depletion. If I have ten dollars and give you five, I have five. My giving money both changes you and costs me. But Wisdom effects changes in others without loss. A common example of undiminished giving was the knowledge of a subject that a good teacher has. When she imparts this to her students, she does not lose a

36. The notion of undiminished giving is discussed, with copious references to ancient sources, in Dodds, *Proclus*, 213–14. Its theological applications have been explored recently by Ayres in "The Holy Spirit." The doctrine of the Integral Omnipresence of Being was apparently first worked out by the third-century Neoplatonist Plotinus as a way of solving the "sailcloth dilemma" from Plato's *Parmenides*: see Plotinus, *Ennead* 6.4–5. For elucidation, see Strange, "Plotinus' Account."

37. Wisdom (*sophia*) is feminine in Greek.

proportionate amount.[38] According to the doctrine of the integral omnipresence of being, God—the one who truly is—is present to physical reality not in separate bits, but integrally. For physical things to be what they are requires some participation in God's reality; but God's reality is not apportioned out among them; immaterial being is present indivisibly in each physical thing. All of this is applied to the Spirit in Basil's homily. Because the Spirit is simple and indivisible, the Spirit is both nowhere and everywhere. But the Spirit is everywhere *entirely*, that is, it is not the case that part of the Spirit is with one person and another part with someone else. We might use the metaphor of "participation" for sharing in the Spirit, but this does not mean that each person receives a *part*.

Second, as in *Against Eunomius* 3.4, Basil draws an idea from Origen and makes it his own. It was Origen who first drew attention to the language of the Spirit's will in 1 Corinthians 12:11 and John 3:8. For Origen, these texts showed that the Spirit is not merely a facet or "mode" of God or a metaphor for God's activity in the world, as the monarchians and Sabellians taught. For Basil, to say the Spirit does as it wishes does not merely prove that it is not identical to the Father and the Son; it also shows that the Spirit is not a servant—one of the "ministering spirits" (Heb 1:14).[39]

38. Basil invokes this stock example in *Eun.* 2.16.

39. Basil clearly refers to this passage when he says that the Spirit does not administer blessings "as a servant" (*leitourgikōs*). The Greek in Heb 1:14 is *leitourgika pneumata*. See also *Spir.* 19.50. Already in *Eun.* 2(.20), Basil argued that the Son is not one of the ministering spirits. Eunomius had referred to the Only-Begotten as God's "most perfect minister" (*Apol.* 15). In Basil's pneumatological works (beginning with *Eun.* 3.2), he applies this point to the Spirit. Due to the tradition of taking the OT theophanies as appearances of the Son, and

Third, Basil uses the category of "economic" sending for the Spirit. Basil had used this language of the Son. Here he extends it. Basil claims that just as the sending of the Son for our salvation does not negate the Son's glory, so too for the Spirit. The Spirit is sent (passive). But the Spirit acts freely (active). Being free and authoritative by nature, the Spirit is unlike fire or the sun, which act upon us "automatically." This qualifies the language of sending: this is no longer a reason for thinking that the Spirit is inferior to God.

Taken together, these points have monumental consequences. Whereas Eunomius or the Pneumatomachians would have seen the Spirit solely as a messenger who is sent in order to draw us beyond itself to God, Basil envisions that the Spirit *is itself what it freely gives*. All analogies fail for this mysterious presence that is simultaneously and without any division the life of God within all Christians.

So what would the monk have found so disturbing about Basil's pneumatology? If he "slurred" over the Spirit, it was not because he lacked a compelling vision of the Spirit's uncreated nature and the ways in which the Spirit is both Giver and Gift in the economy of salvation. It was because he did not say, in so many words, that the Spirit is "God." Nazianzen very much shared the monk's disappointment with Basil, despite his affected "defense" of Basil in his *ep.* 58. Through Gregory, Basil became known for his "economy"—the word meaning "prudent reserve" or "fuzziness" in this context—and this has appeared to many observers since as the defining characteristic of his pneumatology, as if Basil's point were to *deny* that the Spirit is

---

due to passages like Isa 9:5, Basil is in fact more willing to use "angel" as a term for the Son than for the Spirit; see *Eun.* 2.18.

God, or at least to be deliberately equivocal on the matter.[40] We have seen that, quite to the contrary, Basil was piercingly and consistently clear on the Spirit's nature. Being in itself what it is sent to give, the Spirit is not one of the heavenly powers or angels. As for the line of criticism represented by his friend and the anonymous monk, Basil never dignified it with a sustained theological response. His letter back to Gregory treats the monk's report as just another example of slander against him, not serious theology. His proposed remedy is for Gregory to come and spend time with him—a request never fulfilled.[41] The awkward power imbalance of a metropolitan and his subordinate bishop had driven a permanent wedge between the two friends.

40. Nazianzen also discusses Basil's "economy" in his public declarations on the Spirit in *or.* 43.68–69. See below, p. 145.

41. Basil, *ep.* 71.

SIX

On the Holy Spirit

If Basil largely ignored Nazianzen's criticism, the same cannot be said for the "Pneumatomachian" criticism, which prompted Basil to write his major work *On the Holy Spirit*. Oddly enough, the immediate impetus for this writing was again dissenters—presumably from the "Pneumatomachian" party—who were present at the liturgy. Some scholars have speculated that this was the feast of the same St Eupsychius, two years later (September 7, 374). Once again, we cannot affirm this with any certainty. We know that Basil caused an uproar in the crowd at a liturgical celebration when he used two doxologies: first "To God the Father, along with the Son, *with* the Holy Spirit," then the more traditional "To God the Father, through the Son, *in* the Holy Spirit." To some, the two were not complimentary—as Basil thought they were[1]—but mutually contradictory. The

1. See *Spir.* 27.68, where Basil says of the two doxologies: "It remains to be said again where they agree with one another and where

former doxology ("with the Spirit") implies that the Spirit is the *object* of worship and not merely the one "in whom" we worship. Although the Spirit had long been honored by the Church, for some Christians the idea of explicit worship of the Spirit went too far.

The uproar was a manifestation of the debate between Basil and Eustathius, which had been brewing since 372. As noted already, previous attempts to bring about a reconciliation between the two were marred by mutual suspicion and accusations.[2] Now Basil would have to publish his thoughts on the matter, and for this, he has a friendly audience. The work *On the Holy Spirit* is addressed to his friend and spiritual "son" Amphilochius. Though Basil's opponents are answered at length, the work itself is not directed at them. Amphilochius has asked him to write this, and he does so, praising Amphilochius for fulfilling the Lord's command to seek in hopes of finding, despite living in a confusing and troubled time for the churches.

The seemingly haphazard and repetitious order of *On the Holy Spirit* can frustrate the reader. We might begin, then, by simply outlining its contents.[3]

1	Prefatory remarks to Amphilochius
2–8	Remarks on the use of prepositions ("from," "through," "with," and "in")

they differ. It is not that they oppose each other as contradictory. Rather, each introduces its own meaning into true religion. For 'in' speaks primarily in relation to us, whereas 'with' proclaims the communion of the Spirit with God."

2. See Basil, *ep.* 125 (AD 372), the context for which is described in *epp.* 130, 244.

3. Note that the work has been divided by modern editors into chapters and paragraphs. It is standard practice to cite both for precision, for instance, *Spir.* 9.22. This is not the 22nd paragraph of chapter 9, but rather paragraph 22, which happens also to be part of chapter 9.

9	"Common concepts" of the Spirit
10–29	Response to objections
30	Lament on the sad state of the churches

Rather than walking through the entire work, we will highlight its broad themes, filling out our analysis with more in-depth examinations of a few passages. At one level, the argument of *On the Holy Spirit* is simple: the Spirit is to be glorified as Lord because of what the Spirit does. That is, from the Spirit's activities, we can learn something of what the Spirit is. Specifically, we are to learn to "classify" it "with" (*synarithmein*) the Father and Son in our thoughts and in our worship; the baptismal formula of Matthew 28:19, Basil contends, directly supports such co-ordination. While this is an accurate description, Basil insists that we place this "learning" into proper context. We must actually begin with some sense of the Spirit's nature before we can understand the Spirit's actions properly. Throughout the work, Basil's principal goal is to bring the reader back to the basics, to what we already believe about the Spirit. He believes that, if we attend to those obvious points which a Christian simply *must* acknowledge about the nature and activities of the Spirit, then the glorification of the Spirit along with the Father and the Son will likewise be obvious.[4]

4. It is sometimes claimed that Basil argues the other way around: namely, that because we glorify the Spirit together with the Father and the Son—for instance, in the liturgical prayer at baptism—we can infer that the Spirit is divine by nature. That is, divinity actually follows from glorification. While it is true that Basil places a great deal of weight on the Church's *lex orandi*, it is inaccurate to claim that the doctrine of the Spirit's divinity simply follows from this for him. For a version of this interpretation, see Meredith, *Cappadocians*, 32–33. Basil actually tends to argue from the Spirit's nature to the Spirit's glorification, or, perhaps better, argues that the two approaches cannot be divorced in the sense that proclaiming the Spirit's nature is glorifying the Spirit.

This marks something of an advance from what Basil said in *Against Eunomius*, where the Spirit's nature and activities do not imply that the Spirit's dignity is equal with the Father and the Son.

Basil's opponents insisted on using a single preposition for each divine Person. Against this wooden approach to language, in chapters 2–8 Basil underscores the elasticity of prepositions in Scripture.[5] While these chapters contain much interesting material, we will pass them by for now. The treatise on the Spirit properly speaking begins at chapter 9. There, Basil outlines what he calls the "common concepts" of the Spirit. In the debate with Eunomius, "common concepts" referred usually to wisdom accessible to all humans.[6] In *Spir.* 9, it refers to ideas generated—in principle in anyone's mind—by Christian sources, whether biblical or non-biblical.[7] These are concepts of the Spirit that Basil presumes are recognizable to any reflective Christian. The non-controversial character of this section is important to bear in mind. Basil wants us to reflect on what we think when we hear biblical titles for the Spirit such as "Spirit of God," "Spirit of truth, who proceeds from the Father," "Righteous Spirit," "Ruling Spirit," and "Holy Spirit."

5. Basil traces his opponents' wooden approach to liturgical grammar to the influence either of Eunomius' teacher Aetius or of pagan philosophy. Quite independently of Basil, some scholars have accused certain late ancient philosophers of dabbling in a "metaphysics of prepositions."

6. Though see *Eun.* 2.25, where Basil speaks of a "common preconception that exists similarly *in all Christians*" (italics mine).

7. *Spir.* 9.22: "Let us now examine the character of our common notions about the Spirit, both those which we have assembled from the scriptures on him and those which we have received from the unwritten teaching of the fathers."

> Proceeding in our thoughts to what is supreme, we are compelled to think of a being perceptible by the mind alone,[8] infinite in power, unlimited in grandeur, unmeasured by times or ages, generous with the good things it has. All who are in need of sanctification turn to it, all who live virtuously desire it, as if they were watered by its inspiration and helped on their way to the goal which is appropriate to them and in accordance with nature. It perfects others, but needs nothing. It lives, not needing to be restored, but supplying life to others. It does not expand bit-by-bit, but is at once complete, abiding in itself and present everywhere. It is the origin of sanctification. It is light perceptible by the mind alone,[9] which of its own accord grants a certain perspicuity, so to speak, to every rational power in its search for the truth. It is unapproachable in nature, but discernable through its goodness. It fills all things with its power, though only those who are worthy participate in it—and it is not partaken of by a single measure, but distributes its activity *in proportion to faith* (Rom 12:6). Simple in nature, it is diverse in its powers. It is wholly present to each and is wholly present everywhere. It is divided without suffering and partaken of completely. Take the sun's ray as an illustration: although its charm is present to each person who enjoys it as if to him alone, it also shines on the earth and the sea, and is mixed with the air. In the same way too, although the Spirit is present to each of those who can receive it, as if to him alone, it sends forth grace which is sufficient and full for all. Those who partake of it enjoy

8. In Greek, *noeran ousian*, "intellectual substance." This is opposed to being perceptible by the five senses.

9. In Greek, *noēton phōs*, "intelligible light," that is, light that is not perceptible by the senses.

> it according to the capacity, not of its power, but of their nature.[10]

The passage is rhetorically powerful, but it raises questions. First, there is the question of Basil's use of philosophical sources here. *On the Holy Spirit* 9 is the one place in Basil's corpus where scholars have with some confidence detected the (possibly indirect) influence of the Neoplatonist philosopher Plotinus.[11] Basil has taken Plotinus's description of Beauty and applied it to the Spirit. The effect is stunning: just as one cannot "know" Beauty without desiring it, so too with the Spirit. As Beauty is not exhausted by being shared in by countless individual beautiful things and people, so too with sharing in the Spirit.

But why would Basil use such ideas? The answer becomes clear when we look at a passage later in the work.

> Each of the heavenly powers is believed to be in a circumscribed place. For the angel who stood beside Cornelius was not simultaneously with Philip. Nor did the one who spoke with Zachariah from the altar at the same time occupy his own station in heaven. Yet, the Spirit is believed to be active at once in Habakkuk and in Daniel at Babylon, and to be with Jeremiah in prison and with Ezekiel at the Chebar. For *The Spirit of the Lord fills the world* (Ws 1:7). And, *Where can I go from your Spirit, and where can I flee from your face?* (Ps 138:7 (LXX)). And the prophet says, *Therefore I am with you, says the Lord, and my Spirit remains in your midst* (Hag 2:4–5). How should we think of the nature of the one who is both present everywhere and is with God? Did our account show that it belongs to the nature which

10. *Spir.* 9.22.
11. Rist, "Basil's 'Neoplatonism,'" at 199–202 and 207–8.

> encompasses everything or to the nature which is contained in specific places, like the angels' nature?[12]

Basil again uses agreed-upon points—an angel "is believed" to be confined to a single location at a time, whereas the Spirit "is believed" to be omnipresent and with God—to secure agreement on the controversial issue. For Basil, such shared beliefs show that the Spirit is "divine in nature."[13] As divine and omnipresent, the Spirit is distinct from the angelic order. Consequently, the Spirit deserves to be glorified as divine. This shows again the interconnection between belief and worship. The purpose in understanding the Spirit's nature, power, and activities is not simply to get certain "facts" about the Spirit right. To acknowledge the Spirit's properties *is already* to worship: "For my part, I would maintain that glorifying the Spirit is nothing other than enumerating the wonders which belong to it."[14]

For Basil, we cannot separate the question of the Spirit's role in inspiring human lives from the question of the Spirit's nature; these questions are distinct, but interconnected. In *Spir.* 19.48–49, Basil suggests a three-fold distinction of biblical language about the Spirit's glory: (1) titles of the Spirit—that is, names which describe what the Spirit is by nature; (2) the Spirit's activities; and (3) the Spirit's acts of kindness towards us and towards the entire creation. Once again, Basil writes that the Spirit is holy and good by nature—indeed holiness and goodness *are* the Spirit's nature and essence. This means that the Spirit's nature is none other than the divine nature itself. So, when the Spirit acts in our world, it is not to be thought of as

12. *Spir.* 23.54. For more on the angels, see *Spir.* 16.38.

13. *Spir.* 23.54.

14. *Spir.* 23.54. Basil earlier made the same point in reference to glorifying Christ (*Spir.* 8.17).

diminished; it remains what it is by nature as it shares that nature with us.

We must keep this in mind as we read passages about the Spirit illuminating our minds. Basil's opponents reasoned that if the Spirit is principally to be thought of as doing God's work "*in* us," then he is not with God, and thus not equal in honor.[15] Like Origen and even like his own opponents, Basil often speaks in *On the Holy Spirit* as if the Spirit's work is primarily a matter of teaching and empowering the faithful.[16] The Spirit enables a unique "spiritual contemplation," as one turns from the letter to the spirit of the Scriptures.[17] The Spirit is present fully only to Christ's disciples, as Jesus' farewell discourse in John's Gospel shows. But this is not evidence of the Spirit's inferiority. In fact, as John's Gospel also clearly implies, the very same is true of the Father and the Son. There, "the world" cannot receive the Father or his Son; only Jesus' friends can do so. Thus, Basil argues, the inaccessibility of the Spirit to those outside of Christ is another point of *similarity* with the Father and the Son.[18] But, even more than this similarity, we must remember that when the Spirit illuminates, it does so "in itself," as Basil expresses in a passage which is a masterpiece of Trinitarian theology:

> When, through the illuminating power, we gaze upon the invisible image of God, and through it are led to

15. One of their arguments along these lines was based on Rom 8:26–27, where the Spirit is said to intercede on our behalf. See *Spir.* 19.50.

16. See esp. *Spir.* 16.38: "The revelation of mysteries appertains particularly to the Spirit."

17. *Spir.* 21.52. In context, Basil is offering an interpretation of 2 Cor 3.

18. *Spir.* 22.53.

> the vision of the archetype who is beyond beautiful, the *Spirit of knowledge* (Is 11:2) is present there, inseparable from him, *in itself* providing the power to behold[19] the image to those in love with the vision of the truth—not making this manifestation from an external source, but *in itself* leading to recognition. For as *no one knows the Father except the Son* (Mt 11:27), so too *no one can say "Jesus is Lord," unless in the Holy Spirit* (1 Cor 12:3). Now it does not say "through the Spirit," but *in the Spirit*. Moreover, *God is Spirit, and those who worship him must worship in Spirit and truth* (Jn 4:24). Similarly, it is written, *In your light we shall see light* (Ps 35:10 (LXX)/36:9), that is, in the illumination of the Spirit, *the true light who enlightens everyone who comes into the world* (John 1:9).[20] Therefore, it shows *in itself* the glory of the Only-Begotten and grants *in itself* the knowledge of God to the true worshippers. So then, the way to knowledge of God runs from the one Spirit through the one Son to the one Father. And, conversely, natu-

19. The word translated "behold" here (*epoptikēn*) was technical in late ancient Christianity and philosophy. It originated in the Eleusinian Mysteries, where it referred to knowledge reserved for initiates. Beginning with Plutarch the pagan and the Christian Clement of Alexandria, "epoptics" denoted the final stage in the philosophical curriculum: ethics—physics—epoptics. In the last stage, we go "beyond things seen and contemplate somewhat of things divine and heavenly, beholding them with the mind alone, for they are beyond the range of bodily sight" (Origen, *Commentary on the Song of Songs*, prologue.3 (trans. by R. P. Lawson, 40). For Basil's use of "epoptic" together with the contemplation granted by the Spirit, see Basil's *Spir.* 22.53 and *ep.* 233.1. Basil refers to the curriculum in *Hom. Ps.* 32 7 (trans. Way, 240) and *Hom. Ps.* 44 9 (trans. Way, 291).

20. Gregory of Nazianzus's doctrine of the Spirit, as presented in his 5th Theological Oration, begins with this application of John 1:9 to the Spirit. Nazianzen also throughout his work applies Psalm 35:10 (LXX) to the Spirit, leading one recent scholar of Nazianzen to take the verse as his subtitle: Beeley, *Gregory of Nazianzus on the Trinity and the Knowledge of God: "In Your Light We Shall See Light."*

> ral goodness, holiness by nature, and royal dignity proceed from the Father through the Only-begotten, to the Spirit. In this way, the *hypostases* are confessed and the pious dogma of the monarchy is not overturned.[21]

The divine nature and dignity proceed from the Father, through the Son, to the Spirit; human knowledge of God, which is rooted in love of the truth, proceeds in the opposite direction. The Spirit plays an indispensable role. We recall from *Against Eunomius* that, for Basil, the "invisible image" of God—the revealer of God—is God's Son. Here, Basil argues that the Spirit grants the "power to behold" this image and, through it, God, the "archetype who is beyond beautiful." The vision of God is fully Trinitarian. One commentator has argued that 1 Corinthians 12:3, quoted here, provides the central biblical idea behind Basil's pneumatology.[22] This conveys an important insight, but it must be qualified. While all parties would have granted that the Spirit enables the knowledge of and confession of Christ as Lord, Basil insists that the Spirit's illuminating work is done *in itself*. Basil's point is that the Spirit is itself light (albeit immaterial light, perceptible by the mind alone). The Spirit is not merely a reflection of the light of a "higher" principle. The Spirit is not carrying out a task assigned to it; it is the illumination it imparts. Thus, in order to understand the Spirit's work in imparting knowledge, we must first perceive, insofar as we are able, the Spirit's nature. At the beginning of the passage Basil says that

21. *Spir.* 18.47. "Monarchy" in this context means "a single first principle," and refers to the teaching that God the Father is the origin of the Son and the Spirit, and through them of the world. Compare *Spir.* 26.64.

22. Hildebrand, *Trinitarian Theology*, 173–87.

the Spirit is not only the illumination which enables the vision of God, it also the object of the vision ("the *Spirit of knowledge* is present there, inseparable from [the image]"). When we see God, we do so through the Spirit; we also see the Spirit. If we are prepared to grant these points, we must give up thinking of the Spirit by analogy with the angels.[23]

With his notion of "spiritual contemplation," Basil clearly implies—following Paul here—that the illumination of the Spirit is necessary for understanding the scriptures rightly. But he goes further than this. In perhaps the most famous section of *On the Holy Spirit*, Basil argues that we should not think that genuine, apostolic tradition is confined to what is written. It also embraces unwritten customs, of which he lists several: the sign of the cross, facing east during prayer, the words of invocation (*epiklēsis*) at the showing forth of the Eucharistic bread and the cup of blessing, anointing with oil, the triple immersion at baptism, as well as the baptismal renunciation of Satan and his angels. What the apostles passed on in secret Basil calls "dogma" (teaching); what they proclaimed openly, he calls "kerygma" (preaching).[24] Concealing the dogmas was not an end in itself, but rather served the same function Origen ascribed to the mysteriousness of scripture: we are led, through the obscurity of our tradition, to become active

23. That Basil's opponents thought this way is clear from their use of 1 Tim 5:21 (on which, see *Spir*. 13:29). See also *Spir*. 23.54. Another of Basil's key arguments against angelic pneumatology is his appeal to the Spirit's unity or monadic character. This appears already in *Eun*. 3.7 and again in *Spir*. 18.44–45. The latter passage, we might note, entered into monastic lectionaries. It is occasionally read at the night prayer vigil of the Carthusian order, as can be seen in Philip Gröning's documentary film *Into Great Silence*.

24. *Spir*. 27.66. In other works, Basil did not consistently maintain this distinction, which appears to have been formulated in an ad hoc fashion while writing *Spir*. See Fedwick, *Church and Charisma*, 73.

seekers for the hidden wisdom contained therein. Nor are the parts passed over in silence trivial. Even the confession of the Trinity is "unwritten" in this sense, and this profession of faith, which is closely modeled on the baptismal formula of Matthew 28:19, is the source of the Christian life.[25] There are *constitutive* parts of the Christian faith which are not expressly stated in scripture, but which only become clear later. Accordingly, the objection to Basil's doxology as "unscriptural" loses its force.

There remains the question of the Spirit's role in creating the physical world. Remember that Basil's opponents denied the Spirit is Creator. Basil always insisted that the Spirit is involved in creation, but the question is "involved in what way?" In *On the Holy Spirit*, Basil largely repeats the account of creation he offered in *Eun.* 3: the Spirit perfects the single divine act of creation, and does so by confirming—that is, sanctifying—the heavenly powers.[26] Late in his life, Basil preached a series of sermons *On the Six Days of Creation* in Genesis, which go somewhat further. Basil claims he has learned to interpret Genesis 1:2, "And the Spirit of God was stirring above the waters" from an unnamed Syrian, whose language (Syriac) is closer to Hebrew. Basil contends that the original meaning of "stirring above" was more like "warming with fostering care," like a "bird brooding upon eggs and imparting some vital power to them as they are being warmed." For Basil, this striking image shows—over against the Pneumatomachians—"that

25. *Spir.* 27.67; cp. *Eun.* 3.5.

26. *Spir.* 16.38, again with reference to Psalm 32:6 (LXX). See also Basil's *Hom. Ps.* 32 (trans. Way, 234–35) for a similar treatment of the verse: "The Word, the Master Craftsman and Creator of the universe, gave entrance into existence to the angels; the Holy Spirit added holiness to them."

the Spirit is not lacking in the creative power."[27] The Spirit is active, whereas the creation is passive. The Spirit gives life which creation needs. This stops short of saying that the Spirit creates *ex nihilo*—that the Spirit brings the creation into being from absolutely nothing. Yet, in Basil's mind it secured the crucial points: the Spirit is inseparable in nature, activity, and dignity from the Father and the Son; the Spirit, while active in our world, is on the other side of an absolute gulf between the divinity and the creation.

27. Basil, *Hex*. 2.6 (trans. Clarke, 30–31, altered).

SEVEN

Christ's Saving Economy: Basil Confronts Apollinarius

From his early dispute with Eunomius, Basil had drawn one moral: bad doctrine results from asking frivolous questions in the face of divine mystery. It is a point he never tired of repeating. Yet, the specific doctrinal issues shifted somewhat over his career. It was not only that he transferred his attention to the Spirit's divinity, as we have seen. Even the christological issues changed. Put in Basil's terms, the christological dispute with Eunomius was largely over "theology," that is, the eternal divinity of the only-begotten Son of God. This issue did not die out. Although Eunomius was in exile, Homoian theology remained regnant in the eastern Roman Empire. But Basil's focus turned increasingly to disputed questions regarding the "economy," the saving life of the divine Son in the flesh, as well as his passion and resurrection. The question was how the divine Son shared human nature. In this chapter, I will discuss

Basil's emerging response, late in his life, to Apollinarius of Laodicea's Christology. Basil responds to Apollinarius's theology in *Homily* 27 (*On the Holy Birth of Christ*) and in a handful of letters.[1] While scholars have been unwilling to assign a year to the homily, it likely comes from roughly the same time as the anti-Apollinarian letters, which were written in 376–77. In these works, we see Basil's early anti-Eunomian model being put to the test. He views those who would ask questions about the saving economy just like those who do so about the theology; they should be content with "the simplicity of the faith." And yet, in addressing their concerns, Basil could not help but engage in innovative thinking himself.

Preaching was one of his tasks as presbyter and later as bishop of Caesarea. He seems to have covered every topic from drunkenness to local martyrs to the creation story. His moral sermons contain piercing analyses of such passions as anger and envy. A handful of Basil's surviving sermons deal with doctrinal issues. While some of Basil's sermons have long been available in English translation, several are in the process of being translated and published by Mark DelCogliano.[2] In one such sermon, which Professor DelCogliano has graciously made available to me in advance of publication, Basil discusses the "Holy Birth of Christ."[3] While we do not know the year in which Basil delivered this address, we know from the sermon itself that it was given at the feast of the Theophany on January 6. This

1. Basil, *epp*. 236 (to Amphilochius), 258 (to Epiphanius), 260 (to bishop Optimus), 261 (to the people of Sozopolis), 262 (to the monk Urbicus), 263 (to the Western bishops), and 265 (to Eulogius, Alexander, and Harpocration, exiled bishops of Egypt).

2. See the section Works by Basil for details.

3. Basil, *hom*. 27, *On the Holy Birth of Christ*.

feast celebrated the "manifestation of God" in the flesh, focusing particularly on the birth of Jesus and early events in his life, up to and including his baptism. A separate feast of the Nativity on December 25 was not established in the churches of the eastern Roman Empire until shortly after Basil's death.

Although Basil's theme is Christ's birth from Mary, he begins with Christ's eternal "birth" (or "begetting") from the Father. Christian faith acknowledges both births. When we try to understand either, however, we are brought to depths that our minds cannot fathom. What is it to say the Son is eternally born from the Father? Or that the same one was born in time from a virgin? Some are tempted to claim that that they have understood the Father's eternal, timeless begetting of the Son, by capturing it in a simple verbal formula or thinking of it in terms familiar to us as a temporal process. Basil counsels instead to "revere it in silence." Do not ask when it happened, or how. Do not think it was like a human birth. Even if we could understand it, words would fail to describe it.[4]

The homily continues with the birth of Christ in time as a human: "God is upon the earth. God is among human beings." This is different from God giving the Law to Moses, or God speaking to the prophets. In Christ, "God is in flesh." And he is not in flesh as something alien to himself: "he possesses humanity as connatural and united to himself." In so doing, "he restores all humanity to himself through flesh the same as ours in kind."[5]

4. As DelCogliano notes in his forthcoming translation, the limited ability of language to express thought is an idea Basil invokes already in an early letter to Gregory Nazianzen (*ep*. 7).

5. By emphasizing that Christ's flesh was of the same kind as ours, Basil was implicitly arguing against the Apollinarians, who believed he possessed heavenly flesh.

But how? Basil uses one of his favorite analogies: the Word's presence in Christ's flesh is like fire heating iron. The major point of the analogy here is to say that fire has a causal effect on iron without itself being affected. Fire changes iron: it makes it hot. But fire does not cease to be what it is in so doing. Its power is not diminished when it heats the iron, and yet "the whole of it fills whatever shares in it." Similarly,

> God the Word was not moved out of himself when *he dwelt among us* (John 1:14). Nor did he undergo a change when *the Word became flesh* (John 1:14). Heaven was not deprived of what it contained, and earth received the heavenly one in its embraces. Do not suppose that divinity fell. . . . Do not imagine that the divinity was altered when it was transferred into flesh. For the immortal is immutable.

Scholars often assert that to speak of God, as Basil did, as self-sufficient, indivisible, and unchanging is to adapt uncritically a conceptual idiom that is foreign to biblical faith. For Basil, however, such language provides the only fully coherent way of talking about the incarnation. Just as with the Spirit, Basil uses the ideas of undiminished giving and the integral omnipresence of being to describe the Word's economic mission. For Basil, these notions frame how we should think of the Word becoming human. The Word is undiminished in its gift of life to us: it becomes flesh and effects changes in humanity without itself experiencing any loss of its fullness. It is integrally (that is, entirely) present in Christ's flesh: this is the point of saying that the "whole" of the fire is shared by the iron. Here, a physical thing (fire) is used as an analogy for an immaterial reality, the Word. One might think that, in the incarnation, one part of the Word is in heaven and another part in Jesus. But this would be a misunderstanding. The Word is entirely in Christ's flesh, though without ceasing to be the Word: both parts of this are important. Think of the alternatives. On one hand, let us imagine that John's Gospel stated that *part* of the Word became flesh. We could ask, "Why not all? Is there some barrier set up by the flesh that prevents the Word from dwelling in it? How does the 'part' we know through Christ relate to the other 'part,' which remained in heaven?" On the other hand, let us imagine that the Word became entirely present in Jesus, but that in so doing it changed fundamentally. We could not then claim that our redemption occurs through the same Word through whom God created the world, to echo the famous phrase of Athanasius in his *On the Incarnation*.[6]

The doctrine of the incarnation is far more radical than the idea of some portion of the deity inhabiting a human, like a case of spirit possession. God the Word does not "shrink" to fit into Jesus. The doctrine of the incarnation is that the Word—the Creator of the universe—is in every way united to humanity in Jesus. It is interesting to note that the philosophically oriented notion of God appears in Basil's preaching. Yet, just like with his doctrinal treatises, Basil is not trying to introduce metaphysics for its own sake; he wishes his listeners to focus ever more carefully on the Incarnation. The ideas of undiminished giving and the integral omnipresence of being help to clarify what the Incarnation is *not*. Christ is fully Word and fully human, *not* some hybrid of partial God and partial human.

6. Athanasius, *On the Incarnation* 1, repeated *passim*. Basil may or may not have known Athanasius's work; regardless, he surely shared Athanasius's emphasis upon the consistency, indeed the identity, between the agent of creation and redemption.

Basil goes through many of the familiar topics of what we call the Christmas story. He comments on Mary's virginity, on the angels, the shepherds, and the visitation of the magi. Throughout, however, he never strays far from his aim to cultivate in the listener the proper attitude to the mysterious wonder of the Incarnation. He returns to the theme as he concludes: "While the magi adore him, Christians inquire: how can God be in flesh? What sort of flesh does he have? Was the humanity complete or incomplete?" Idle curiosity drowns out reverent silence. There should be no question what the real *point* of the Theophany is: it is the story of "God in a small infant," a tale in which "the divine power was manifested through the human body . . . and shines upon those who have the eyes of their heart purified."

When Basil draws his contrast between the reverent magi and the inquiring Christians, he appears to deny the very value of theological questioning altogether. Regardless of whether one agrees with Basil, one must distinguish Basil's rhetoric from his actual practice. On the surface, Basil, like many Christian authors of his day, draws a firm line between piety and inquiry, casting a suspicious glance at the latter. It is understandable: there is such a thing as idle curiosity, and the seemingly endless doctrinal debates of Basil's day could appear at least as tedious to participants as they seem to modern readers. But Basil only seems to censure curiosity when it leads in a doctrinal direction of which he disapproves. This is clear with the anti-Eunomian literature. In the Theophany sermon just quoted, it seems that he has a new target, Apollinarius of Laodicea. Sometime around 360, before his ordination, Basil had corresponded with Apollinarius.[7] Not unlike Basil, whose

7. See above, p. 62, n. 28.

father taught rhetoric, Apollinarius was the son of a well-known Christian grammarian (also named Apollinarius). By 360, the younger Apollinarius had become a Christian bishop who was noted for his erudition and his support of the Nicene faith. By the later years of Basil's life, however, Apollinarius had fallen under suspicion for his christological doctrine.[8]

Two of Apollinarius's ideas drew the most attention. The first had to do with Christ's flesh. Apollinarius denied that Christ's flesh was the same as ours; he and some of his followers seem to have viewed Christ as a "heavenly man" who descended with glowing flesh. In his earthly life, Christ's flesh is not the same as ours. In Basil's phrase, the Apollinarians needlessly speculate: "What kind of flesh does he have?" Our modern assumption is that human flesh comes in only one variety—the kind we have—and that incarnation implies that Christ had this kind. Yet, Christians since Paul have spoken of risen bodies as "heavenly" or "spiritual bodies" and therefore as different from the bodies we currently have (1 Cor 15:35–57). Perhaps Christ's flesh, even before his passion and resurrection, was spiritual. After all, in the same context, Paul said that Christ was a "man from heaven." These are questions that Basil would prefer we did not entertain, not simply because they represent fruitless speculation, but more importantly because Apollinarius's answer removes Christ's likeness to us. It destroys Christ's mediatorial role. For Basil, Christ is *both* God *and* human, not something in between.

Apollinarius's idea might seem strange to us, but it clearly gained support, for instance among Christians in

8. The doctrine later ascribed to his name is already noted as problematic in the *Tome to the Antiochenes* 7 from Athanasius, though his name is not mentioned there.

Sozopolis, a city in Pisidia. In 377, Basil wrote a letter to the Christians there, underscoring the need for Christ's flesh to be the same as ours:

> For if the flesh which was ruled over by death was one thing, and that which was assumed by the Lord was another, death would not have ceased accomplishing its own ends, nor would the sufferings of the God-bearing flesh have been our gain; He would not have killed sin in the flesh; we who died in Adam would not have been made to live in Christ; that which had fallen apart would not have been put together again; that which had been thrown down and broken would not have been set aright again; that which was alienated by the serpent's deceit would not have been joined to God. For all these things are destroyed by those who say that the Lord had a heavenly body when He was present.[9]

A particular understanding of redemption stands behind the passage. Although it was common in Basil's day, it is less so today and deserves comment. It starts with a simple presupposition: humanity is in some physical way a unity. What happened to Adam as a result of the devil's deceit affects all of us. Given this unity, what happens to Christ is able to touch all of us. In his flesh, Christ conquered the death that humanity inherited from Adam. Like his contemporaries, Basil advocated an understanding of Christ's salvific work that modern scholars have labeled "Christus Victor": Christ saves by conquering death and the devil. This victory occurred especially in Christ's own dying and rising, which showed death to be powerless. But Christ could not be the victor so if his flesh were of a different kind than ours. His share in our nature has to be

9. Basil, *ep*. 261 (D 4:77–79); similarly in *ep*. 262.

total in order for him to mend our broken flesh, which had become liable to death, and to unite it to God.

Apollinarius's second controversial idea was that he denied that Christ had a rational mind, so that his humanity was "incomplete," as Basil put it.[10] In response, Basil asserts that Christ's humanity was more than mere flesh. This is apparent in a letter to Amphilochius, in which he tries to reclaim certain "heretical" proof-texts such as Mark 13:32 (about the Son's ignorance of the Day of Judgment, a favorite verse of the radical Homoians) and John 4:7 (in which Jesus is portrayed as thirsty):

> Then, moreover, to one who examines intelligently, the Lord often discourses with men from his human side also; for example, *Give me to drink* (John 4:7) is an expression of the Lord satisfying his bodily need. And yet he who asked was not flesh without soul, but Godhead which had made use of flesh endowed with soul.[11]

This affirms that Christ's flesh was "endowed with soul." He elaborates on this point in his letter to the people of Sozopolis. There, he draws a threefold distinction. We can consider a human from three angles: as mere flesh, as flesh endowed with soul, and as soul making use of flesh. The most we can say about mere flesh is that it is divisible—it suffers by what physically happens to it. Flesh endowed with soul is flesh that is alive. As such, it also becomes weary, feels hunger and thirst (as in John 4:7), and feels physical pain. Christ shared all of these feelings with us. But

10. Basil did not dwell on this as thoroughly as certain other anti-Apollinarian writers of his day did; e.g., Epiphanius, *Panarion* 77; and G. Naz., *epp.* 101, 102. Both of these authors also deal extensively with Apollinarius's views of Christ's heavenly flesh.

11. Basil, *ep.* 236 (D 3:391).

proper to a soul making use of a body are forms of psychological suffering: grief, anxiety, and cares. Some of these are natural and in no way sinful. Christ experienced these. He grieved when his friend died. But other psychological cares are contrary to our nature, such as anxiety over amassing political power or wealth. Christ did not share these. This is how Basil understands Romans 8:3 (Christ "was made in the likeness of sinful flesh") and 1 Peter 2:22 ("yet he did no sin"). The Apollinarians had used the former verse to argue that Christ was merely *like* us, not one of us.

For Basil, it was crucial to affirm that Christ endured the same struggles we do. This again has to do with how Basil understood Christ's saving work. We saw above that Christ conquered death in his flesh. But that is only side of the story: he also conquered sin. To do that, he himself had to have flesh endowed with soul and soul using a body. In showing us a life like ours, yet sinless, he purified our flesh. Basil combines his two points—Christ's defeat of death and of sin:

> [J]ust as death, that is, death in the flesh, which was transmitted to us through Adam, was swallowed up by the divine nature, so too sin was destroyed by the righteousness which was in Christ Jesus, so that we in the resurrection will resume flesh that is neither liable to death nor subject to sin.[12]

With this meditation on Christ's twofold work of salvation, Basil goes further than anything he had previously written on the topic. Over against Apollinarius, Basil affirms Christ as perfect God and perfect man, who conquers death and destroys sin, thus giving us hope of a restored life in the flesh without the limitations and fears we currently experience. Basil's own theology was shaped

12. Basil, *ep.* 261 (D 4:83, modified).

by his encounter with Apollinarian ideas. In a letter from 376, Basil disavowed all speculation into the incarnation, preferring to content himself with what the Nicene Creed had said.[13] But he did not stick to that. When faced with what he considered the pastoral necessity of preaching and of counseling by letter the Christians in Sozopolis, he elaborated his own anti-Apollinarian theology. He portrayed himself as simply reproducing "the traditions of the fathers."[14] And his teaching did contain traditional elements. But he underestimated his own originality. Faced with Apollinarius, Basil offered a nuanced appreciation of the divine economy of the Son of God, who in his humanity purified our embodied state of both death and sin, a state we hope to attain in the next life.

To fight openly against Apollinarius was especially painful for Basil.[15] Early in his career, he had corresponded with Apollinarius—something that Basil's opponents in Sebasteia never tired of mentioning in their propaganda against Basil. Apollinarius had distinguished himself early in his career as a supporter of Nicaea. There is a sense of bewilderment and sadness in anti-Apollinarian works by Athanasius, Epiphanius, and Basil. Still, each of these felt the need to break with Apollinarius for his doctrine on the economy. In 376, the feud became even more pressing. It was in that year that the Apollinarians proposed Vitalis as bishop of Antioch, further exacerbating the already-tense

13. Basil, *ep.* 258. The disavowal of speculation has to do with the irenic intent of this letter to Epiphanius.

14. Basil, *ep.* 261 (D 4:83).

15. See Basil, *epp.* 263, 265. The doctrines attributed to Apollinarius in these two letters are more wide-ranging than we have discussed. Basil mentions his Trinitarian error (implicit Sabellianism) and his teaching on the ongoing relevance of Jewish law and customs for Christians.

problem there. Vitalis technically made it a four-way split. Thus, the fight with Apollinarius and his followers had implications not only for doctrine but also for communion among the churches.

EIGHT

Basil's Final Years

The final years of Basil's life were tumultuous. Basil repeatedly compared the state of the churches in the East to a ship on stormy seas, tottering at the brink of shipwreck. In 373, Valens initiated a purge of Nicene bishops from their sees. Egypt and Syria were particularly hard hit, with dozens of bishops and probably thousands of monks and clerics expelled. Across the empire, monks were pressed into hard labor. Basil's longtime friend and supporter Eusebius of Samosata was ordered to abandon his see in 374. Trumped-up charges were brought against Gregory of Nyssa and he was forced out of his city. Homoian replacements were imposed in all these cases. The well-connected Basil, who had a prior relationship with Valens, escaped the persecutions. Nevertheless, for the final five years of his life, his network must have seemed in shambles.[1] In a letter from 376, he wistfully remarked that his one relief was his

1. See Lenski, *Failure of Empire*, 255–63.

repeated bodily illness, "because of which I am convinced that I shall remain for no long time in this unhappy life."[2]

In addition to imperial pressure, there were the doctrinal disagreements we have studied at length. According to some scholars, in his final years, Basil's Trinitarian theology took a decisive step forward, with the moves he made in these years solidifying his position as the architect of the pro-Nicene confession of three hypostases and one substance. It is certainly true that, in these years, his various projects began to be brought together into a whole vision. Starting around 376, and in response to new allegations against his teaching, he found a new rhetoric. He now portrayed proper Trinitarian theology as a kind of mean between Sabellianism on one hand and Eunomianism on the other.[3] Because of its emphasis upon divine unity, Basil now contentiously likens Sabellianism to Judaism; Basil speaks of Eunomianism's separable divine substances as a form of polytheism. The first fails to recognize the proper, distinguishing characteristics of the three hypostases; the second fails to recognize their shared substance and their inseparability in all that they do. The rhetoric of orthodoxy as a mean between "Judaism" and "polytheism" would reappear in the writings of the two Gregories. Already in *Against Eunomius* Basil had spoken of the Son sharing in the Father's divine substance. In 376, he explicitly extended this formal analysis to the Spirit as well. He still did not speak of the Spirit as *homoousios* with the Father or the Son. But he had a handy rule he could teach friends: "as

2. Basil, *ep*. 212 (D 3:221).

3. Casting one's own position as a mean between extremes was common. In a letter from 376, Basil criticized other Christians, perhaps Pneumatomachians and/or moderate Homoians, who portrayed themselves as occupying the mean between the "Anhomoians" and the Nicenes: Basil, *ep*. 212.

the common is to the particular, so is the substance to the hypostasis."[4] He also began to see "hypostasis" as a better anti-Sabellian word than *prosōpon*: words he had previously used as synonyms.[5] So, at the same time, he was seeking a clearer anti-Sabellian formula, and a clearer statement of the Spirit's full share in the divine nature. But, as we saw in the case of the Son, this language of shared substance is rather formal. While it gives us certain rules for speaking, it only takes us so far. It would be wrong to present it as the heart of Basil's thought on the Trinity. For that, Basil continues to use the by now familiar language of Trinitarian illumination, balanced with the incomprehensibility of God.

Even more intractable than outright doctrinal disagreement was the problem of schism among those who, in some important respects at least, were of like mind. The situation in Antioch, where there were three claimants to the episcopal throne (four if we count the Apollinarian Vitalis), had to be dealt with. Disunity of this kind could not be addressed with a mere theological treatise. It required people to recognize one another as part of a common Christian fellowship. The difficulty was enhanced by the regular presence of Valens and his court in Antioch from 372 until 378. Valens's favored Homoian bishops—Euzoius until his death in 376, when Dorotheus succeeded him—could not be easily dethroned. To Basil, however, their doctrinal beliefs clearly disqualified them; similarly with Vitalis. But the split between supporters of Paulinus and Meletius was far more sensitive. Both affirmed the faith of Nicaea—and did not carry it in the Apollinarian direction

4. Basil, *ep*. 214 (to Count Terentius) and, probably a little earlier that same year, *ep*. 236 (to Amphilochius).

5. Hildebrand, *Trinitarian Theology*, 82–101.

that Vitalis favored. While they understood its creed somewhat differently, many, including Basil, viewed the differences between Paulinus and Meletius as not necessarily posing obstacles to full communion.

Basil was unambiguous in his support for Meletius. Six letters from Basil to Meletius survive, all from the period of Basil's episcopacy.[6] While Meletius had been placed on Antioch's episcopal throne by the hated Council of Constantinople of 360, Basil could not bring himself to blame him for this. As for Paulinus, Basil did not necessarily find him unworthy of office. At least that is what Basil said in a conciliatory letter to Epiphanius of Salamis in 376.[7] Basil was not entirely forthcoming: in the following year, he would accuse Paulinus of "being inclined toward the teachings of Marcellus," and hence toward Sabellianism.[8] This would escalate the conflict into an outright doctrinal dispute. But there was also the matter of established ties of communion. Prior to Paulinus's consecration in 362, the see of Caesarea, under Dianius's guidance, had established communion with Meletius. Basil had not seen anything blameworthy in Meletius to prompt him to alter this status.[9] Meletius's subsequent move in a Nicene direction theologically did not hurt matters, either.

6. Basil, *epp.* 57, 68, 89, 129, 120, 216.

7. Basil, *ep.* 258.

8. Basil, *ep.* 263 (AD 377). Paulinus had also, Basil charges, accepted followers of Marcellus into communion without proper discrimination. Also in 377, Basil lodges the same allegation against certain exiled Egyptian bishops living in Palestine (*ep.* 265). See also the same year's *ep.* 266 to Peter of Alexandria, where Basil strives to enlist Peter in the task of reconciling the Marcellans into communion. This very task would be assigned to Basil's brother Gregory at a synod of pro-Nicene bishops in Antioch in 379, after Basil's death.

9. Basil, *ep.* 258.

In 371, Basil began a letter-writing campaign to enlist the bishops of Alexandria and Rome for Meletius's cause. This was a hard sell. Hurt by the consecration of Paulinus, which he thought (falsely, it seems) Athanasius had engineered, Meletius had refused to recognize Athanasius as being a bishop in communion with the church of Antioch. In 372, Basil urged him to send Athanasius a letter initiating a reconciliation, but to no avail.[10] Athanasius died in 373 and his pro-Nicene successor Peter was in exile in Rome. Damasus, Liberius's successor as pope in Rome, recognized Paulinus as rightful bishop of Antioch. Despite the difficulties, some progress was made toward mutual recognition. Perhaps in response to Basil's entreaties, Damasus issued a document, known to posterity as *Confidimus quidem*. Basil expresses some degree of approval of this. However, during his lifetime, Basil's campaign for a united Nicene front in Antioch, centered on Meletius as the sole Nicene bishop, never succeeded. Basil grew increasingly disillusioned with Damasus, whom he spoke of in scathing terms as power-hungry, proud, and prone to flattery.

During Basil's final years, his reputation in the Christian world was not without ambiguity. In Asia Minor, even in his family's homeland of Pontus, many were troubled by his severing of ties with Eustathius. Further away, we have seen that Athanasius never directly responded to Basil's attempts to enroll him in support of Meletius in Antioch. However, he seems to have acknowledged Basil as someone who was not to be crossed lightly. In a letter to Palladius, Athanasius spoke of Basil as "a glory to the church." Yet, he probably perceived Basil as too compromising with former "Homoians" such as Meletius. In a comparison both laudatory and subtly critical, he likens Basil's accommodating

10. Basil, *ep.* 89.

tendencies to Paul, who became "weak for the sake of the weak."[11] We might compare the monk whom Gregory of Nazianzus met, who mocked Basil's doctrine of the Spirit as politically correct whitewashing rather than courageous Trinitarianism.

Indeed, it could be argued that the image of Basil as *the* Trinitarian stalwart of the East in the 370s is the product of the historical circumstance that he happened to be one of the very few prominent supporters of Nicaea in the Eastern Mediterranean left in office during Valens' purges, and surely the most intellectually gifted and well connected.[12] Basil's survival in office may have been unlikely, but it was no accident.

Probably shortly before Basil's death in 378, Eunomius finally unveiled his response to Basil's *Against Eunomius.* His attack was not only doctrinal, but also personal, calling Basil a liar and a coward, "scared at the sound of the door."[13] A fifth-century follower of Eunomius named Philostorgius says, quite improbably, that Basil actually received a copy and died of grief from having been so roundly refuted. He probably never saw it.

Despite the breakdown in Basil's relationships with Eustathius and Gregory of Nazianzus, he was not without friends and allies. His younger brother Gregory remained loyal, as did Eusebius of Samosata, whom Basil viewed as a spiritual father and Amphilochius, Basil's spiritual son. In ill health, he continued to correspond with his large network. He was a pastor to the end. In what was perhaps his final letter, he consoles the grieving wife of a recently

11. Athanasius, *ep.* 63 (*NPNF*² 4:580).

12. See G. Nyssa, *Eun.* 1.143, who of course attributes this to Basil's courage and strength of character in face of persecution.

13. Eunomius, *AA*, quoted by G. Nyssa, *Eun.* 1.138 (Hall, 55).

deceased general named Arinthaeus.[14] Arinthaeus had distinguished himself by his service under Constantius, Julian, and Valens.[15] He had supported the church for years. Basil had written to him in the past, requesting him to use his influence on behalf of a certain churchman named Eusebius, perhaps the bishop of Samosata, who had been exiled under Valens.[16] On his deathbed, Arinthaeus had been baptized. Basil reminds his wife—who had presumably been a Christian for much longer—of the hope this should bring. He does not condemn her sorrow, though he does urge fortitude and moderation in grieving. Much of this counsel would apply to any grieving person. Yet, Arinthaeus's rank is never far below the surface of Basil's remarks. In his letter of consolation, there is a rather easy—too easy, one might think—transfer of the general's earthly, secular status to his spiritual reward: as "great in the present life," Arinthaeus would be "great in the life to come," says Basil. The letter is a reminder that Christian pastoral concern was becoming increasingly public and thus linked to the affairs of the empire's elite citizens like Arinthaeus. It was the same concern that compelled Basil to write his treatises and sermons on the Trinity, as well as to perform his charitable work. Early in his life, he had longed to escape public affairs altogether. His sense of Christian duty and

14. Basil, *ep.* 269.

15. For another example of Basil's correspondence with soldiers, see *ep.* 106. Acquaintance with this unnamed soldier was a great blessing, Basil writes, since it proved to him that "even in military life one may preserve the perfection of love for God" (D 2:203).

16. Basil, *ep.* 179. The letter must be read together with *epp.* 177, 178. Fedwick suggests the Eusebius mentioned in the latter two is Eusebius of Samosata: *Basil of Caesarea* 1:12 nn. 63–64. Others claim it is a different Eusebius: Pouchet, *Basile le Grand*, 309; Van Dam, *Kingdom of Snow*, 233 n. 16.

the changing circumstances of the church had conspired to make this impossible. Soon, Basil himself would die. Like the general, though for quite different reasons, Basil would be posthumously eulogized as "great" in this life and in the life to come.

Conclusion

In his letters, Basil frequently complained of illness. We do not know the cause of Basil's death, but he and those closest to him must have seen it coming. He died surrounded by disciples, one of whom he made sure to ordain to the priesthood before he passed. He had been bishop of Caesarea for eight years,[1] its leading pastor for longer. He had often spoken of his old age, but was not yet fifty.

There has been some debate over the date of his death. A persuasive case has been made for sometime around September 378.[2] The oft-cited day of January 1, 379, is based on the assumption that the feast date promoted by Gregory of Nyssa was meant to commemorate Basil's exact date of death, but Gregory does not himself place the death on that day. While the autumn of 378 is likely, we cannot specify the date with any certainty. We are more certain about the context. From Gregory of Nazianzus's oration on his friend, we learn that Basil died in Caesarea, and that the entire city—Christians, pagans, and Jews—grieved. The outpouring of emotion was so strong that some members of the nameless throng were killed during his funeral

1. G. Nyssa, *Life of Macrina* (Callahan, 173).

2. Silvas, *Gregory of Nyssa: The Letters*, 32–39, following the work of Pierre Maraval and J.-R. Pouchet.

procession, trampled as they sought to touch Basil's holy body.[3] A grief-stricken Gregory of Nyssa retreated to Annisa to inform the family.[4]

Probably earlier that same year, Gregory of Nyssa had been allowed to return from the exiled imposed upon him by Valens. Also freed from exile was Eunomius, who was finally able to leave the island of Naxos. He had recently published his *Apology for the Apology*. Shortly after Basil's death, the work found its way into the hands of Gregory of Nyssa. While still in mourning, he would be asked to defend Basil; his brother Peter confirmed his inclination to show no mercy.[5]

Eunomius himself moved to Constantinople, where he sought influential patrons for his teaching. However, with the accession of Theodosius—a Spanish general who was also an ardent and intolerant pro-Nicene Christian—as emperor of the east in 379, it was the supporters of Nicaea who took the lead. At the Council of Constantinople summoned by Theodosius in 381, "Eunomians" were listed among the condemned heretics. This did not immediately stop Eunomius. In 383, he was still pressing his cause in Constantinople, this time at a "Council of the Heresies," at which Theodosius sought (perhaps naively) to give all the heretics an opportunity to present a statement of faith. Eunomius offered one, which is still extant. It was refuted by Gregory of Nyssa. Although Theodosius forbade heretical assemblies, Eunomius stayed on in and around Constantinople, continuing to attract disciples. In

3. G. Naz., *or.* 43.78–80.

4. G. Nyssa, *On the Soul and the Resurrection* (Callahan, 198); however, the timeline in Gregory's *Life of Macrina* (Callahan, 173) seems to contradict this narrative.

5. G. Nyssa, *ep.* 29.4.

389, Theodosius learned that certain "servants of his bed chamber" were Eunomians, and banished Eunomius, first to the legionary outpost city of Halmyris along the Danube, later transferring him to Caesarea in Cappadocia.[6] As you might expect, he was not received favorably there. He went to live on his own property nearby at Dacora. There, he continued to lead his followers and to attract visitors such as the twenty-year-old Philostorgius, who would later write a pro-Eunomian *History of the Church*. In 395, he was ousted from Caesarea by Arcadius, Theodosius's successor, and forced to move to a rural monastic community near Tyana, where he died in 396/97.

The tide had turned irrevocably toward the Nicene cause. The alliance of East and West, which Basil had hoped to build, came to fruition not long after his death. In 379, with Theodosius's support, a synod of pro-Nicene bishops met in Antioch. Led by Meletius, they acknowledged communion with Damasus of Rome. There remained unresolved issues between East and West and among Easterners themselves, but the alliance forged at Antioch in 379 enabled the pro-Nicene Council of Constantinople in 381. From Antioch, Gregory of Nazianzus was sent to Constantinople to lead the pro-Nicene Christian minority there. Gregory of Nyssa was dispatched to reconcile the lingering followers of Marcellus in Ancyra to the pro-Nicene cause. Basil's influence surely lies somewhere behind the broad (though not unanimous) approval of the doctrine articulated by the Council of Constantinople in 381, although the council's creed was likely not directly drawing on his writings. Basil has justly been remembered through the ages as a father of Christian orthodoxy.

6. Philostorgius, *CH* 10.6.

But it is worth pausing to ask exactly how this image of Basil was constructed. Recall that it was not the only portrait available: even apart from Eunomius, who unsurprisingly attempted a character assassination, in the previous chapter we noted ambiguities in the assessment of Basil offered by Athanasius, as well as by many in Asia Minor. In one sense, Basil's reputation was a function of the speeches of praise offered on him after his death by his brother Gregory and his friend Gregory, as well as his brother's theological defense of him in his own work *Against Eunomius*.[7] In Caesarea on January 1, 381 (or perhaps 380), Gregory of Nyssa delivered a magnificent *Encomium on His Brother Basil*. Gregory portrays Basil as an equal of the apostles and martyrs. In so doing, Gregory helped to solidify this date as the Feast of St. Basil the Great. He was extolled by his brother for his ascetic virtue, his boldness before Valens and his vicars, his famine relief efforts, and above all for his teaching on the Trinity. Gregory also suggests that Basil's talk of divine illumination was not simply a matter of theory or of eschatological expectation: "at night as he prayed in the house the glow of a light came on him. That light was something immaterial, illuminating his room by divine power, enkindled by no material thing."[8] Basil would become one of the first non-martyrs to merit an annual festival.[9] In 382 or 383, Gregory of Nazianzus went

7. Basil's friend Amphilochius perhaps offered an encomium on him. One fragment of such a work survives and is attributed to him, but it is considered inauthentic.

8. G. Nyssa, *Encomium on His Brother Basil* 21. Two points are worth noting by way of context: first, Basil never claims such experience for himself; second, Gregory intends a rhetorical comparison of Basil's experience with Moses' vision at the burning bush.

9. Basil himself attested to the devotion given to a non-martyr saint in Cappadocia. In his to Ambrose of Milan (*ep*. 197), Basil

to Caesarea to deliver his *Oration on Basil.*[10] Although the two had never reconciled, Gregory heaped wistful praise upon his fallen friend. He even co-opted Basil for his own cause, claiming that his friend had privately taught that the Spirit is of the same substance (*homoousion*) with the Father, even though for political reasons he had not done so publicly.[11] Gregory portrayed himself as treating the Caesarean audience to the "real story" behind Basil's frustrating "economy." Each of the Gregories remembered Basil in a self-serving way. Gregory of Nyssa, in particular, clearly wanted to be viewed as Basil's successor. Each of them also exaggerated Basil's virtues. Yet, there can be no doubt that, without their tributes, it is unlikely that we would remember Basil as we do. We should not discount either Gregory's sincerity in praising Basil.

Amidst the formulaic praise of Basil, Gregory of Nazianzus offers precious glimpses of Basil's personality. Basil was bearded and pale and walked with an odd gait. He spoke thoughtfully and with such hesitation that some thought him to be depressed. He could be clever and funny at a moment's notice: "his improvisations were much more

---

described the sending of the relics of St. Dionysius of Milan back to Milan, as per Ambrose's request. St. Dionysius had not been given up without a fight. In Cappadocia, Dionysius, through his relics, had been viewed by the local Christians as a "father and protector." He had been given honor "worthy of a martyr" (D 3: 97), a phrase that indicates the novelty of the veneration of non-martyrs. Basil's letter does not mention an annual festival for Dionysius, but this does not mean there was none.

10. For suggestions as to the date and occasion, see McGuckin, *Saint Gregory of Nazianzus*, 372–74.

11. G. Naz., *or.* 43.69.

precious and brilliant than the laboured efforts of other men."[12]

Despite the importance of the two Gregories' memorials of Basil, his posthumous reputation was not solely a projection of others' ideals onto him. Citizens of Caesarea had visible evidence of his charitable work in the Basileias. His writings left an indelible imprint on subsequent Christian thought. They clearly influenced the voluminous writings of the two Gregories, even if each developed his own distinctive profile as a theologian. In the decades after Basil's death, any differences that might originally have divided Basil and the Gregories were ironed out and they were read as common defenders of orthodoxy against heresy. In the fifth century, this assumption took physical form in books called *florilegia*, collections of passages by important church fathers arranged by topic. Seeking to show the common mind of the fathers, compilers of these collections excerpted passages from Basil, Amphilochius, the two Gregories, Athanasius, Didymus, and others. Theodoret of Cyrrhus, for instance, used Basil as an authority in this way in his christological dialogue *Eranistes* from around 447. This use of citations from previous post-scriptural Christian authorities to buttress one's argument has its origin in Basil himself, who employed it in his *On the Holy Spirit*. Within seventy-five years of his death, Basil's texts were read as authorities, much as he had read his own predecessors; Basil was not beyond being questioned, but he was taken with a *prima facie* seriousness. Basil's works were read and cited by theologians throughout the history of the Byzantine Empire (the continuation of the Eastern Roman Empire centered on Constantinople and lasting through 1453). The list of those who cited him includes

12. G. Naz., *or.* 43.77.

Severus of Antioch, Dorotheos of Gaza, John of Damascus, Photius, Symeon the New Theologian, and Gregory Palamas. Gregory of Nyssa's report of Basil experiencing visible divine illumination during his prayers no doubt heightened the positive reception of his work among the latter two, who emphasized such experience of the divine glory and of the Spirit's eternal light as the height of Christian spirituality. On the more popular level, Basil was known through iconography and through the Anaphora or Divine Liturgy, which bears his name and which many scholars believe to contain a core that goes back to Basil himself. On various annual occasions, including Sundays in Lent and Basil's feast day, this liturgy is used to this day by Orthodox Christians of the Byzantine Rite.

Basil's influence on historic Christianity was not confined to the Greek East. Within decades of his death, translations of some of his works were made into Latin. Most influential in the West were his monastic rules, his *Homilies on the Six Days of Creation*, and various other homilies. Augustine discussed the work on Genesis in his work on the same topic. In the *Rule of St. Benedict*, the architect of Western monasticism, the "rule of our holy father Basil" is mentioned alongside John Cassian's works as recommended reading for monks.[13] Benedict's phrase for the divine office, "the work of God," comes from Basil, who used it more expansively to include also manual labor.[14] The scholastic thinkers in the medieval universities of the West, such as Thomas Aquinas, cited Basil, if at second hand. In 1532, Erasmus of Rotterdam, the great Catholic scholar of the Northern Renaissance, oversaw the publication of the first printed edition of Basil's works; he called

13. *Rule of St Benedict* 73.

14. *SR* 167, 200. See Silvas, *Asketikon*, 363 n. 472.

Basil "the Christian Demosthenes."[15] Numerous editions have appeared since, although we lack properly critical editions for many works.

The scholarly study of Basil is ongoing. One thing is becoming clear: alongside Basil the bishop, the church politician, and the monastic organizer, scholars must appreciate the gifts of Basil the theologian.[16] Of course, Basil's own conviction was that doctrine and the practical matters of Christian living are entirely inseparable from one another.[17] In Basil's day, as in ours, both areas contained disputed questions. Basil's answers to these may not always satisfy us, but I hope we can appreciate his attempts more fully. Within the Christian Scriptures and the subsequent tradition of theology, he discovered seeds of reflection on the most mysterious and controversial of topics. He did so while insisting upon a stance of theological humility: that we not claim to know more about God than we can.

For Basil, the ultimate incomprehensibility of God, the "archetype who is beyond beautiful," does not mean that we throw our hands up and stop trying to know God better and to become more like God.[18] Nor does God's mysteriousness mean that we must invent from scratch our own concepts for God; we might develop some new ones through "conceptualization," but these will simply be new ways of imitating and enacting the biblical *exempla*. In *On the Holy Spirit*, Basil mentions that one's attention

15. Rudberg, "Manuscripts and Editions," 1:56.

16. See DelCogliano, *Basil's Anti-Eunomian Theory*, 266.

17. Among countless examples, see Basil, *ep*. 295 (to monks): "Strictness of life in itself, unenlightened by faith in God, is not beneficial. Nor can the correct confession of faith, which is devoid of good works, bring us to the Lord. Rather, both must go together."

18. *Spir*. 18.47; see pp. 115–17 above.

should extend all the way to the prepositions used in Scripture—this from the same work that revels in the "unwritten" aspects of tradition. Even so, Christians should not expect to find in these prepositions a definitive model for the relations of the Trinity. The trick is to know when rational scrutiny is required and when to bask in the awe of God's glory. The irony, as Basil's late anti-Apollinarian briefs testify, is that theological originality typically comes when one is least attempting it, even when one is rhetorically seeking to deny it at all costs; in sum, when one is most anxious precisely about innovation.

Divine pedagogy ultimately belongs to the Spirit, who instructs and sanctifies even the angels. There is no knowledge of God that does not involve the illumination of the Spirit—the illumination which the Spirit *is* and which it graciously and without any loss grants to the eyes of the soul purified by discipline and attentiveness. To know God involves participating in the glory that is the Spirit's from before the ages alongside the Son and the Father. In the economic mission of Christ and his Spirit, this glory comes from the Father, through the Son, and is given to the faithful in the Spirit, which enables them to behold God in his eternal image, the Son. To know God is to be caught up into this eternal circle.

This need not be understood as occurring only in special "mystical" experiences of direct vision, in which one is transported outside of the limitations of the body and time. God's life has been woven into flesh and time by the economy of Christ and the Spirit, a single mission extended in the tradition of baptism, the celebration of the Eucharist or "mystery of godliness," the regular observance of the hours of prayer, and the steady progression through the cycle of the liturgical year. Basil envisioned a gradual growth in wisdom—moving "from glory to glory"—in the discipline of a life marked by charity, justice, obedience, communion, and right belief. The creeds and summaries of faith which Basil and his contemporaries produced were, in their own estimation, mere starting points for this journey—necessary, it is true, but not to be mistaken for the vision of God to which they meagerly point. In a letter to an otherwise unknown Christian named Eupaterius and his daughter, Basil offered one such summary of faith in the Spirit's divine nature: being "holy by nature," the Spirit deserves our reverence along with the Father and the Son. Undoubtedly, this is an essential point to safeguard. And we have seen the fragile, but real networks of Christian charity established by such exchanges of letters. But the real work, Basil acknowledged, was out of his hands: "from small seeds *you* will cultivate the fullness of right belief, *the Holy Spirit co-operating with you*."[19]

19. Basil, *ep*. 159 (D 2:399, modified, italics mine).

Works by Basil

Title (English)	Greek Edition	English Translation	Date of Writing[1]
Against Eunomius (books 1–3)	Sesboüé, Bernard, with Georges-Matthieu de Durand and Louis Doutreleau, ed. and trans., *Contre Eunome, suivi de Eunome: Apologie* (SC 299, 305; Paris: Cerf, 1982–83)	DelCogliano, Mark, and Andrew Radde-Gallwitz, trans., *Against Eunomius* (FotC 122; Washington, DC: Catholic University of America Press, 2011)	364–65
epistles (368 extant, many dubious or spurious; of especial interest are *ep.* 8, now commonly ascribed to Evagrius Ponticus, and *ep.* 38, ascribed commonly to Gregory of Nyssa)	Yves Courtonne, ed. and trans, *Basile: Lettres*, 3 vols. (Paris: Les Belles Lettres, 1957–66)	D	357–78 (see Fedwick, "Chronology," for dates of individual letters)

1. For further details on dating, an indispensable resource is Paul Jonathan Fedwick, "A Chronology of the Life and Works of Basil of Caesarea," in idem, ed. *Basil of Caesarea*, 1:3–19.

Works by Basil

Title (English)	Greek Edition	English Translation	Date of Writing
homilies 1–9, on the Hexaemeron	Giet, Stanislas, ed. and trans., *Basile de Césarée: Homélies sur L'Hexaéméron*, 2nd ed. (SC 26; Paris: Cerf, 1968)	Jackson, Blomfield, trans., *The Treatise De Spiritu Sancto, the Nine Homilies of the Hexaemeron, and the Letters* (*NPNF*[2] 8; 1895, repr. Peabody, MA: Hendrickson, 1999) 52–107 Way, Agnes Clare, trans., *Exegetic Homilies* (FotC 46. Washington, DC: Catholic University of America Press, 1963) 3–150	378
Homily on Psalm 1	PG 29b	Way, FotC 46, 151–64.	363–78
Homily on Psalm 7	PG 29b	Way, FotC 46, 165–80.	363–78
Homily on Psalm 14, part 1	PG 29b	DelCogliano, Mark, trans., *Basil of Caesarea: On Christian Doctrine and Practice* (Popular Patristics Series; Crestwood, NY: St Vladimir's Seminary Press, forthcoming)	363–78

Title (English)	Greek Edition	English Translation	Date of Writing
Homily on Psalm 14, part 2	PG 29b	FotC 46, 181–92 Schroeder, C. Paul, trans., *On Social Justice* (Popular Patristics Series 38; Crestwood, NY: St Vladimir's Seminary Press, 2009) 89–99	363–78
Homily on Psalm 28	PG 29b	Way, FotC 46, 193–212	363–78
Homily on Psalm 29	PG 29b	Way, FotC 46, 213–26	363–78
Homily on Psalm 32	PG 29b	Way, FotC 46, 227–46	363–78
Homily on Psalm 33	PG 29b	Way, FotC 46, 247–74	363–78
Homily on Psalm 44	PG 29b	Way, FotC 46, 275–96	363–78
Homily on Psalm 45	PG 29b	Way, FotC 46, 297–310	363–78
Homily on Psalm 48	PG 29b	Way, FotC 46, 311–32	363–78
Homily on Psalm 59	PG 29b	Way, FotC 46, 333–40	363–78
Homily on Psalm 61	PG 29b	Way, FotC 46, 341–50	363–78
Homily on Psalm 114	PG 29b	Way, FotC 46, 351–60	363–78
Homily on Psalm 115	PG 29b	DelCogliano, *On Christian Doctrine and Practice*	363–78

Works by Basil

Title (English)	Greek Edition	English Translation	Date of Writing
homily 1, *On Fasting*	PG 31		363–78
homily 2, *On Fasting*	PG 31		363–78
homily 3, *On the Words, "Know Thyself"*	PG 31	Wagner, M. Monica, trans., *Ascetical Works* (FotC 9; Washington, DC: Catholic University of America Press, 1962) 431–46; Harrison, Nonna Verna, trans., *On the Human Condition* (Popular Patristics Series; Crestwood, NY: St Vladimir's Seminary Press, 2005) 93–106	363–78
homily 4, *On Giving Thanks*	PG 31		363–78
homily 5, *On the Martyr Julitta*	PG 31		363–378
homily 6, *On Luke 12:18* ("I will tear down my barns") *and on Avarice*	PG 31	Schroeder, *On Social Justice*, 59–71	363–78, likely 369–70

Title (English)	Greek Edition	English Translation	Date of Writing
homily 7, *On the Rich*	PG 31	Schroeder, *On Social Justice*, 41–58	363–78, perhaps 369–70
homily 8, *In time of Famine and Drought*	PG 31	Holman, Susan R., *The Hungry Are Dying: Beggars and Bishops in Roman Cappadocia* (Oxford Studies in Historical Theology; Oxford: Oxford University Press, 2001) 183–92 Schroeder, *On Social Justice*, 73–88	363–78, likely 369–70
homily 9, *That God Is Not the Author of Evils*	PG 31	Harrison, *On the Human Condition*, 65–80.	363–78, likely 369–70
homily 10, *Against Anger*	PG 31	Wagner, FotC 9, 447–62 Harrison, *On the Human Condition*, 81–93	363–78
homily 11, *On Envy*	PG 31	Wagner, FotC 9, 463–74 DelCogliano, *On Christian Doctrine and Practice*	363–78

Works by Basil

Title (English)	Greek Edition	English Translation	Date of Writing
homily 12, On the beginning of Proverbs	PG 31	DelCogliano, *On Christian Doctrine and Practice*	363–78
homily 13, Exhortation to Holy Baptism	PG 31		363–78
homily 14, On Easter Drunkenness	PG 31		363–78
homily 15, On the Faith	PG 31	DelCogliano, *On Christian Doctrine and Practice*	363–78
homily 16, On the Words, "In the Beginning Was the Word"	PG 31	DelCogliano, *On Christian Doctrine and Practice*	363–78
homily 18, On the Martyr Gordius	PG 31	Allen, Pauline, trans., in Johan Leemans et al., *"Let Us Die That We May Live": Greek Homilies on Christian Martyrs from Asia Minor, Palestine, and Syria (ca. AD 350–AD 450)* (London: Routledge, 2003) 57–67	363–78, perhaps 373

Title (English)	Greek Edition	English Translation	Date of Writing
homily 19, On the Holy Forty Martyrs of Sebasteia	PG 31	Allen, in *"Let Us Die That We May Live"*, 68–76	363–78, perhaps 373
homily 20, On Humility	PG 31	Wagner, FotC 9, 745–86 DelCogliano, *On Christian Doctrine and Practice*	363–78
homily 21, On Detachment from Worldly Goods, and on the Conflagration Started Outside the Church	PG 31	Wagner, FotC 9, 487–506 DelCogliano, *On Christian Doctrine and Practice*	likely 372–73
homily 23, On the holy martyr Mamas	PG 31		363–78
homily 24, Against Sabellians, Arius, and Anomoians	PG 31	DelCogliano, *On Christian Doctrine and Practice*	363–78
homily 26, Delivered in Lakizis	PG 31	DelCogliano, *On Christian Doctrine and Practice*	363–78
homily 27, On the Holy Birth of Christ	PG 31		363–78, likely 376–77

Works by Basil

Title (English)	Greek Edition	English Translation	Date of Writing
homily 29, *Against Those Who Slanderously Say That We Say There Are Three Gods*	PG 31	DelCogliano, *On Christian Doctrine and Practice*	363–78
Longer Responses	PG 31, 89–1052.	Wagner, FotC 9, 223–338; Silvas, Anna M., *The Asketikon of St. Basil the Great* (Oxford Early Christian Studies; Oxford, Oxford University Press, 2005) 153–270	363–78 (see Silvas, *Asketikon* for details on various revisions)
Morals	PG 31, 700–888.	Wagner, FotC 9, 71–206	
On Baptism (2 books)	Umberto Neri, ed. and trans., *Il battesimo* (Testi e ricerche di scienze religiose 12; Brescia: Paideia Editrice, 1976) Neri's Greek text is reprinted, with a French translation, by Jeanne Ducatillon, ed. and trans., *Sur le Baptême* (SC 357; Paris: Cerf, 1989)	Wagner, FotC 9, 339–430	372–75 (Fedwick, "Chronology")

Title (English)	Greek Edition	English Translation	Date of Writing
On the Faith (Preface to *Moral Rules*)	PG 31, 676–92.	Wagner, FotC 9, 57–69	365–72 (Fedwick, "Chronology")
On the Holy Spirit	Benoît Pruche, ed. and trans., *Sur le Saint-Esprit* (SC 17; Paris: Cerf, 2002)	Hildebrand, Stephen M., trans., *On the Holy Spirit* (Yonkers, NY: St Vladimir's Seminary Press, 2011)	375
On the Judgment of God (Preface to *Moral Rules*)	PG 31, 653–76.	Wagner, FotC 9, 37–56	372–75, re-released 376–77
Shorter Responses	PG 31, 1052–1320.	Silvas, *The Asketikon of St Basil the Great*, 271–451	363–78 (see Silvas, *Asketikon* for details on various revisions)
To Young Men on the Value of Greek Literature	Fernand Boulenger, ed. and trans., *Aux jeunes gens*, 2nd ed. (Paris: Les Belles Lettres, 2002)	D 4:379–435	356–78

Primary Sources

For ancient sources cited in the book, I have provided the common English translation of the work's title, together with bibliographical information on an available English translation of the work.

Anonymous

The Book of Steps

ET: *The Book of Steps: The Syriac Liber Graduum*. Translated by Robert A. Kitchen and Martien F. G. Parmentier. Cistercian Studies Series 196. Kalamazoo, MI: Cistercian, 2004.

Athanasius of Alexandria

epistles and *Tome to the Antiochenes*

ET: *St. Athanasius: Select Works and Letters*. Edited by Archibald Robertson. *NPNF*[2] 4. Peabody, MA: Hendrickson Publishers, 1994 [1892].

epistles to Serapion

ET: *Works on the Spirit: Athanasius's Letters to Serapion on the Holy Spirit and Didymus's On the Holy Spirit*. Translated by Mark DelCogliano, Andrew Radde-Gallwitz, and Lewis Ayres. Popular Patristics Series 43. Yonkers, NY: St Vladimir's Seminary Press, 2011.

On the Incarnation

ET (with Greek edition): Athanasius, *Contra Gentes and De Incarnatione*. Edited and translated by Robert W. Thomson. Oxford Early Christian Texts. Oxford:

Clarendon, 1971.

Basil of Caesarea (see the previous section, Works by Basil)

Benedict of Nursia
The Rule of St. Benedict
ET: *The Rule of St. Benedict in English*. Edited by Timothy Fry. Vintage Spiritual Classics. New York: Vintage, 1998.

Cyprian of Carthage
On the Lord's Prayer
ET: Tertullian, Cyprian, and Origen. *On the Lord's Prayer*. Translated by Alistair Stewart-Sykes. Popular Patristics Series. Crestwood, NY: St. Vladimir's Seminary Press, 2004.

Didymus the Blind
On the Holy Spirit
ET: see Athanasius, *epistles to Serapion*.

Epiphanius of Salamis
Medicine-Chest (*Panarion*)
ET: *The Panarion of Epiphanius of Salamis*, vol. 2, *Books II and III (Sects 47–80, De Fide)*. Translated by Frank Williams. Nag Hammadi and Manichaean Studies 35. Leiden: Brill, 1994.

Eunomius of Cyzicus
Apology for the Apology
ET: see Gregory of Nyssa, *Against Eunomius*.

Apology and *Confession of Faith*
ET (with Greek edition): *The Extant Works*. Edited and translated by Richard Paul Vaggione. Oxford Early Christian Texts. Oxford: Clarendon, 1987.

Gregory of Nazianzus
epistles and *oration* 43
ET: *S. Cyril of Jerusalem, S. Gregory Nazianzen*. Translated by Charles Gordon Browne and James Edward Swallow. *NPNF*[2] 7. Peabody, MA: Hendrickson, 1994 [1894].

Gregory of Nyssa

Against Eunomius (3 books)

ET:

Book 1: In *El "Contra Eunomium I" en la Produccion Literaria de Gregorio de Nisa*, translated by Stuart G. Hall, edited by Lucas Mateo-Seco and Juan L. Bastero, 35–138.Colección Teológica 59. Pamplona: Ediciones Universidad de Navarra, 1988.

Book 2: In *Gregory of Nyssa: Contra Eunomium II*, translated by Stuart G. Hall, edited by Lenka Karfíková, Scot Douglass, and Johannes Zachhuber, 59–201. Proceedings of the 10th International Colloquium on Gregory of Nyssa. Supplements to Vigiliae Christianae 82. Leiden: Brill, 2007.

Book 3: In *Gregory of Nyssa: Contra Eunomium III*, translated by Stuart G. Hall, edited by Johan Leemans. Proceedings of the 12th International Colloquium on Gregory of Nyssa. Leiden: Brill, forthcoming.

Encomium on His Brother Basil

ET: *Encomium of Saint Gregory, Bishop of Nyssa, on His Brother Saint Basil, Archbishop of Cappadocian Caesarea*. Translated by James Aloysius Stein. Patristic Studies 17. Washington, DC: Catholic University of America Press, 1928.

homilies on Ecclesiastes

ET: *Gregory of Nyssa: Homilies on Ecclesiastes*. Translated and edited by Stuart G. Hall. Proceedings of the 7th International Colloquium on Gregory of Nyssa. Berlin: de Gruyter, 1993.

epistles

ET: *Gregory of Nyssa: The Letters*. Translated by Anna M. Silvas. Supplements to Vigiliae Christianae 83. Leiden: Brill, 2007.

Life of Macrina and *On the Soul and the Resurrection*

ET: *Ascetical Works*. Translated by Virginia Woods Callahan. FotC 58. Washington, DC: Catholic University of America Press, 1967.

Primary Sources

Hilary of Poitiers

On the Synods

ET: *Hilary of Poitiers, John of Damascus*. Edited by Philip Schaff and Henry Wace. *NPNF*[2] 9. Peabody, MA: Hendrickson, 1994 [1899].

John Cassian

Institutes

ET: *Sulpitius Severus, Vincent of Lerins, John Cassian*. *NPNF*[2] 11. Peabody, MA: Hendrickson, 1994 [orig. pub. 1894].

Justin Martyr

First Apology

ET: *The First and Second Apologies*. Translated by Leslie William Barnard. Ancient Christian Writers 56. New York: Paulist, 1997.

Origen

Commentary on the Song of Songs

ET: Origen. *The Song of Songs: Commentary and Homilies*. Translated by R. P. Lawson. Ancient Christian Writers 26. New York: Newman, 1956.

On First Principles

ET: Origen. *On First Principles: Being Koetschau's Text of the De Principiis*. Translated by G. W. Butterworth. Gloucester, MA: P. Smith, 1973 [1966].

Philostorgius

Church History

ET: *Philostorgius: Church History*. Translated and by Philip R. Amidon. Writings from the Greco-Roman World 23. Atlanta: Society of Biblical Literature, 2007.

Plotinus

Enneads

ET: *Plotinus*. Translated by A. H. Armstrong. 7 vols. Loeb Classical Library 440–45, 468. Cambridge, MA: Harvard University Press, 1966.

Pseudo-Hippolytus
The Apostolic Tradition
ET: Paul F. Bradshaw, Maxwell E. Johnson, and L. Edward Phillips. *The Apostolic Tradition: A Commentary*. Edited by Harold. W. Attridge. Hermeneia. Minneapolis: Fortress, 2002.

Rufinus of Aquileia
Church History
ET: *The Church History of Rufinus of Aquileia, Books 10 and 11*. Translated by Philip R. Amidon. New York: Oxford University Press, 1997.

Socrates
Church History
ET: *Socrates, Sozomenus: Church Histories*. Edited by Philip Schaff and Henry Wace. *NPNP*² 2. Peabody, MA: Hendrickson, 1994 [1890].

Sozomen
Church History
ET: see Socrates, *Church History*.

Tertullian
On the Prayer
ET: see Cyprian, *On the Lord's Prayer*.

Theodoret of Cyrrhus
Church History
ET: *Theodoret, Jerome, Gennadius, Rufinus: Historical Writings, Etc.* Edited by Philip Schaff and Henry Wace. *NPNF*² 3. Peabody, MA: Hendrickson, 1994 [1892].

Secondary Sources

Reference Works and Collections of Essays

Fedwick, Paul Jonathan, editor. *Basil of Caesarea: Christian, Humanist, Ascetic.* 2 vols. Toronto: Pontifical Institute of Mediaeval Studies, 1981.

Fedwick, Paul Jonathan, editor. *Bibliotheca Basiliana Vniversalis.* 5 vols. Turnhout: Brepols, 1996–2004.

Secondary Sources

Ayres, Lewis. "The Holy Spirit as Undiminished Giver: Didymus the Blind's *De Spiritu Sancto* and the Development of Pro-Nicene Pneumatological Traditions." In *The Theology of the Holy Spirit in the Fathers of the Church: The Proceedings of the Seventh International Patristic Conference*, edited by Janet Rutherford and Vincent Twomey, pp. 57–72. Dublin: Four Courts, 2010.

———. *Nicaea and Its Legacy: An Approach to Fourth-Century Trinitarian Theology.* Oxford: Oxford University Press, 2004.

Ayres, Lewis, and Andrew Radde-Gallwitz. "Basil of Caesarea." In *The Cambridge History of Philosophy in Late Antiquity*, edited by Lloyd Gerson, 1:459–70. Cambridge: Cambridge University Press, 2010.

Beeley, Christopher. *Gregory of Nazianzus on the Trinity and the Knowledge of God: "In Your Light We Shall See Light".* Oxford Studies in Historical Theology. Oxford: Oxford University Press, 2008.

Bernardi, Jean. *La prédication des Pères Cappadociens: La prédicateur et son auditoire.* Paris: Presses universitaires de France, 1968.

Bucur, Bogdan. *Angelomorphic Pneumatology: Clement of Alexandria and Other Early Christian Witnesses.* Leiden: Brill, 2009.

Secondary Sources

Clark, Elizabeth A. *Reading Renunciation: Asceticism and Scripture in Early Christianity*. Princeton, NJ: Princeton University Press, 1999.

Corona, Gabriella, editor. *Aelfric's Life of Saint Basil the Great*. Anglo-Saxon Texts 5. Cambridge: D. S. Brewer, 2006.

DelCogliano, Mark. "Basil of Caesarea, Didymus the Blind, and the Anti-Pneumatomachian Exegesis of Amos 4:13 and John 1:3." *Journal of Theological Studies*, n.s., 61 (2010) 644–58.

———. *Basil of Caesarea's Anti-Eunomian Theory of Names: Christian Theology and Late-Antique Philosophy in the Fourth Century Trinitarian Controversy*. Leiden: Brill, 2010.

Dodds, E. R., *Proclus: The Elements of Theology*. Oxford: Clarendon, 1963.

Drake, H. A. "The Impact of Constantine on Christianity." In *The Cambridge Companion to the Age of Constantine*, edited by Noel Lenski, 111–36. Cambridge: Cambridge University Press, 2006.

Drecoll, Volker Henning. *Die Entwicklung der Trinitätslehre des Basilius von Cäsarea: Sein Weg vom Homöusianer zum Neonizäner*. Göttingen: Vandenhoeck & Ruprecht, 1996.

Elm, Susanna. *'Virgins of God': The Making of Asceticism in Late Antiquity*. Oxford: Clarendon, 1994.

Fedwick, Paul Jonathan. *The Church and the Charisma of Leadership in Basil of Caesarea*. Eugene, OR: Wipf and Stock, 2000 [1979].

Hanson, R. P. C. *The Search for the Christian Doctrine of God: The Arian Controversy, 318–381*. Grand Rapids: Baker, 2005 [1988].

Haykin, Michael A. G. "And Who Is the Spirit?: Basil of Caesarea's Letters to the Church at Tarsus." *Vigiliae Christianae* 41 (1987) 377–85.

Hildebrand, Stephen M. *The Trinitarian Theology of Basil of Caesarea: A Synthesis of Greek Thought and Biblical Truth*. Washington, DC: Catholic University of America Press, 2007.

Holman, Susan R. *The Hungry Are Dying: Beggars and Bishops in Roman Cappadocia*. Oxford: Oxford University Press, 2001.

Holmes, Augustine. *A Life Pleasing to God: The Spirituality of the Rules of St. Basil*. Kalamazoo, MI: Cistercian, 2000.

Lenski, Noel. *Failure of Empire: Valens and the Roman State in the Fourth Century A.D.* Berkeley: University of California Press, 2002.

McGuckin, John. *Saint Gregory of Nazianzus: An Intellectual Biography*. Crestwood, NY: St. Vladimir's Seminary Press, 2001.

Meredith, Anthony. *The Cappadocians*. Crestwood, NY: St. Vladimir's Seminary Press, 1995.

Norton, Peter. *Episcopal Elections, 250–600: Hierarchy and Popular Will in Late Antiquity*. Oxford: Oxford University Press, 2007.

Pouchet, J.-R. *Basile le Grand et son univers d'amis d'après sa correspondance: Une stratégie de communion*. Rome: Studia Ephemeridis Augustinianum 36, 1992.

Radde-Gallwitz, Andrew. *Basil of Caesarea, Gregory of Nyssa, and the Transformation of Divine Simplicity*. Oxford: Oxford University Press, 2009.

Rist, John. "Basil's 'Neoplatonism': Its Background and Nature." In *Basil of Caesarea: Christian, Humanist, Ascetic*, edited by Paul Jonathan Fedwick, 1:137–220. Toronto: Pontifical Institute of Medieval Studies, 1981.

Rousseau, Philip. *Basil of Caesarea*. Berkeley: University of California Press, 1994.

Rudberg, Stig Y. "Manuscripts and Editions of the Works of Basil of Caesarea." In *Basil of Caesarea: Christian, Humanist, Ascetic*, edited by Paul Jonathan Fedwick, 1:49–65. Toronto: Pontifical Institute of Medieval Studies, 1981.

Sesboüé, Bernard. *Saint Basile et la Trinité, un acte theologique au IVe siècle: le rôle de Basile de Césarée dans l'élaboration de la doctrine du langage trinitaires*. Paris: Desclée, 1998.

Silvas, Anna M. *The Asketikon of St. Basil the Great*. Oxford: Oxford University Press, 2005.

———. "Edessa to Cassino: The Passage of Basil's *Asketikon* to the West." *Vigiliae Christianae* 36 (2002) 247–59.

———, translator. *Gregory of Nyssa: The Letters*. Leiden: Brill, 2007.

Sterk, Andrea. *Renouncing the World Yet Leading the Church: The Monk-Bishop in Late Antiquity*. Cambridge, MA: Harvard University Press, 2004.

Stramara, Daniel F. "Double Monasticism in the Greek East, Fourth through Eight Centuries." *Journal of Early Christian Studies* 6 (1998) 269–312.

Strange, Steven K. "Plotinus' Account of Participation in *Ennead* VI.4–5." *Journal of the History of Philosophy* 30 (1992) 479–96.

Vaggione, Richard P. *Eunomius of Cyzicus and the Nicene Revolution*. Oxford: Oxford University Press, 2000.

Van Dam, Raymond. *Becoming Christian: The Conversion of Roman Cappadocia*. Philadelphia: University of Pennsylvania Press, 2003.

———. *Families and Friends in Late Roman Cappadocia*. Philadelphia: University of Pennsylvania Press, 2003.

———. *Kingdom of Snow: Roman Rule and Greek Culture in Cappadocia*. Philadelphia: University of Pennsylvania Press, 2002.

Name and Subject Index

Acacius, 46, 49, 59
Aelfric, 9n10, 37n35
Aetius, 46–47, 49, 51, 57, 61–62, 111n5
Ambrose of Milan, 144n9
Amphilochius of Iconium, 9, 18, 100n25, 109, 122n1, 129,135n4, 138, 144n7, 146
Anthimus of Tyana, 95
Antioch (AD 341), Dedication Council of, 46, 60
Antiochene schism, 58–59, 96n15, 131–32, 135–37, 143; *see also* Euzoius, Meletius, Paulinus, Vitalis
Apollinarius of Laodicea, 62n28, 100, 121–22, 126–32
Ariminum (359), Council of, 48
Arius, 43–44, 54n15, 60
Armenia, 3, 6, 26, 95, 99
Athanasius of Alexandria, 44, 46, 48, 56–59, 125, 127n8, 131, 137, 138n11, 144, 146
Athens, xiv, 6, 9, 23–24, 29, 32
Basil of Ancyra, 46–48
Basil of Caesarea
  epp.
    ep. 1, 25–26;
    ep. 2, 25, 29–34
    ep. 7, 123n4
    ep. 9, 65, 67, 96–97
    ep. 14, 28–29
    ep. 27, 94n10
    ep. 37, 28n15, 91n3
    ep. 52, 97–98, 102n30
    ep. 57, 94n11, 136n6
    ep. 68, 136n6
    ep. 71, 107n41
    ep. 89, 136n6, 137n10
    ep. 91, 14–15
    ep. 93, 64n1
    ep. 94, 3, 95n12
    ep. 99, 100n22
    ep. 100, 100n25
    ep. 106, 139n15
    ep. 113, 99n21
    ep. 114, 99n21
    ep. 120, 136n6
    ep. 125, 16n22, 99–100, 102n30, 109n2
    ep. 129, 136n6
    ep. 130, 100n22, 109n2
    ep. 140, 102n30

Basil of Caesarea (*continued*)
ep. *142, 100n25*
ep. *159, 16n22, 102n32, 150*
ep. *160, 25n9*
ep. *176, 95n12*
ep. *177, 139n16*
ep. *178, 139n16*
ep. *179, 139n16*
ep. *197, 144n9*
ep. *200, 100n25*
ep. *204, 22n2*
ep. *207, 27, 79n2*
ep. *210, 16n22, 96n15*
ep. *212, 134nn2–3*
ep. *214, 135n4*
ep. *216, 136n6*
ep. *223, 22n2, 25n10, 28n16, 31–32, 35n30, 41n44, 62n28, 65n4*
ep. *226, 100n23*
ep. *233, 116n19*
ep. *234, 18*
ep. *236, 96n15, 122n1, 129, 135n4*
ep. *244, 26n13, 100n22, 100n24, 109n2*
ep. *252, 100n25*
ep. *258, 96n15, 122n1, 131n13, 136n7, 136n9*
ep. *260, 122n1*
ep. *261, 122n1, 128, 130, 131n14*
ep. *262, 122n1, 128n9*
ep. *263, 122n1, 131n15, 136n8*
ep. *265, 122n1, 131n15, 136n8*
ep. *269, 138–39*
ep. *295, 148n17*
ep. *361, 62n28*
ep. *362, 62n28*
ep. *363, 62n28*
ep. *364, 62n28*
Eun., 7, 10, 42, 50, 54n15, 57n21, 65–89, 96n15, 97, 97n17, 102n30, 105, 105nn38–39, 111, 111n6, 117, 118n23, 119, 134
Hex., 7, 70n12, 119, 120n27, 147
Hom.
Hom. *12, 40n41*
Hom. *15, 101–3*
Hom. *27, 122–26*
Hom. Ps. *32, 30n20, 116n19, 119n26*
Hom. Ps. *44, 116n19*
LR, xi, 7, 31n23, 34n39, 36, 37n36, 38nn37–38, 39n39, 41n43, 78–79, 86n12
Spir., 7, 11, 80, 86n13, 96n15, 97, 105n39, 108–20, 148n18
SR, 7, 31n23, 36, 39–40, 41nn43–44, 147n14
To Young Men on the Value of Greek Literature, 30–31
Basil the Elder (father of Basil), 23
Benedict of Nursia, 37, 147
Book of Steps, 38n38
Clement of Alexandria, 116n19
Constantinople, 6, 23, 32, 47, 142–43, 146; *see also* Constantinople (AD 360), Council of; Constantinople (AD 381), Council of

Constantinople (AD 360), Council of, 46, 47n5, 49, 51, 58, 60–61, 64, 100, 136
Constantinople (AD 381), Council of, 79, 102n30, 142–43
Constantius II (emperor), xiv, 43, 48–49, 59, 61, 63, 139
Cyprian of Carthage, 78n1
Damasus of Rome, 137, 143; *see also* Antiochene schism
Demophilus of Constantinople, 61
Dianius of Caesarea, 27, 50, 64, 136
Didymus the Blind, 82n8, 89, 103n34, 104, 146
Dionysius of Alexandria, 96–97
Dionysius of Milan, 144n9
Emmelia (mother of Basil), 22
Epiphanius of Salamis, 47, 53n12, 63, 122n1, 129n10, 131, 131n13, 136
Erasmus of Rotterdam, 147
Eudoxius, 46, 49, 51, 58, 60–62
Eunomius of Cyzicus, 42–43, 46, 48–62, 65–68, 71–76, 81–82, 85–89, 96, 105n39, 106, 111, 111n5, 121, 138, 142–44
Eupsychius, 100, 100n25, 101n28, 108
Eusebius of Caesarea (in Cappadocia; Basil's predecessor), 64, 90–92,
Eusebius of Caesarea (in Palestine; the church historian, apologist, and theologian), 8, 45, 46
Eusebius of Nicomedia, 45
Eusebius of Samosata, 60, 93–94, 100n25, 133, 138–39
Eustathius of Sebasteia, 25–26, 28, 31, 35–37, 42, 47, 60, 62n28, 63, 65, 98–100, 109, 137–38
Euzoius, 46, 58–59, 135
Epiphany, Feast of the, *See* Theophany, Feast of the
Firmilian of Caesarea, 78n1
George of Alexandria, 46, 57–58
George of Laodicea, 47, 47n4
Gibbon, Edward, 48
Gregory of Nazianzus, 5, 11, 17, 23n3, 24, 35, 90, 93, 93n5, 95–96, 100, 101n28, 106, 108, 123n4, 138, 143–45
Epp., 8, 93nn6–7, 94n9, 101n26, 129n10
Or. 43, 2n3, 3n4, 8, 22n1, 23n4, 24n6, 25n10, 95n14, 107n40, 141, 142n3, 144–45, 145n11, 146n12
Theological Orations, 116n20
Gregory of Nyssa, 8, 11, 23, 23n3, 35, 95, 133, 141–45, 147
Encomium on his brother Basil, 8, 91, 144, 144n8,
Epp., 20n25, 142n5
Eun., 2n2, 9, 50, 52n9, 52n11, 55n16, 138nn12–13

Gregory of Nyssa (*continued*)
Hom. 4 Eccl., 28n15
Life of Holy Macrina, 8, 22n1, 24n7, 28, 141n1
On the Soul and the Resurrection, 142n4
Gregory the Elder (father of Gregory of Nazianzus), 24, 93–94
Himerius, 9, 24
Homoians, 43, 45–49, 51, 57–61, 63, 90, 121, 129, 133–35, 137; *see also* Acacius; Constantinople (AD 360), Council of; Constantius II (emperor); Eudoxius; Eunomius of Cyzicus; Valens (emperor)
Homoiousians, 12, 43, 45–49, 55, 58–63, 66–67, 98
Homoousios (of the same substance); *see* Nicaea (AD 325), Council and Creed of
John Cassian, 78n1, 147
John Chrysostom, 5
Julian (emperor), xiv, 59, 61, 100n25, 139
Justin Martyr, 32n26
Libanius, 9, 23
Liberius of Rome, 60, 137
Lucifer of Cagliari, 58
Macrina (sister of Basil), 8, 22, 28, 35; *see also* Gregory of Nyssa, *Life of Holy Macrina*
Macrina the Elder (grandmother of Basil), 22
Marcellus of Ancyra, 44, 46, 48, 62, 136, 143
Maximinus Daia, 22
Meletius, 46, 58–60, 63, 94, 96n15, 135–37, 143; *see also* Antiochene schism
Modestus, 2
Naucratius (brother of Basil), 23, 35
Nicaea (AD 325), Council and Creed of, 1, 2, 4, 9, 12–15, 38n37, 43–45, 48, 55, 57–63, 66–67, 79, 92, 94, 99–100, 102, 127, 131, 133–38, 142–43
Origen of Alexandria, 19, 33, 38n37, 52, 66, 72, 82, 86, 104–5, 115, 116n19, 118
Paulinus, 58–59, 96n15, 135–37; *see also* Antiochene schism
Peter of Alexandria, 136n8, 137
Peter of Sebasteia (brother of Basil), 20n25, 23, 142
Philo of Alexandria, 104
Philostorgius, 9, 138, 143
Plotinus, 104n36, 113
Pneumatomachians, 47n5, 99n21, 106, 108, 119, 134n3; *see also* Eustathius of Sebasteia
Prohaeresius, 9, 24
Rufinus 9, 35–37, 38n37
CH 35–36
Sabellius and Sabellianism, 16, 44–45, 55, 62, 96, 98–100, 105, 131n15, 134–36

Sasima, 95; *see also* Gregory of Nazianzus
Seleucia (AD 359), Council of, 48–49
Shepherd of Hermas, 80–81
Sirmium (AD 357), Council of, 45–46; *see also* Homoians
Socrates (church historian), 9
    CH, 1n1, 47n5, 49n9, 59n22, 60nn23–24
Sozomen, 9
    CH, 47n5, 59n22, 60nn23–25, 100n25
Tertullian, 78n1
Theodoret of Cyrrhus, 9, 146
    CH, 3n5, 4n7, 9, 61n27
Theodosius (emperor), xv, 142–43
Theodotus of Nicopolis, 99
Theophany, Feast of the, 1, 61, 122, 126
Theophany of the Son in the Old Testament, 73, 105n39
Theosebeia, 23n3
Tyana, xv, 60, 95, 100, 143
Valens (bishop), 46
Valens (emperor), xiv–xv, 1–4, 17, 49, 59–61, 63, 90, 95, 133, 135, 138, 139, 142, 144
Valentinian (emperor), 1, 60
Vitalis, 131–32, 135–36; *see also* Antiochene schism

Scripture Index

OLD TESTAMENT

Genesis

1:2 119

Exodus

3:14 30, 53, 53n14, 73

1 Samuel

19:20 2–3

Job

33:4 86

Psalms (LXX numbering)

18:9 40
32:6 86, 119n26
35:10 74, 116, 116n20
50:12–13 79, 102n32
109:3 72n14
138:7 113
142:10 40, 79, 84, 102n32

Proverbs

8:22 33, 56

Isaiah

9:5 105n39

Daniel

1:4 30

Amos

4:13 82n8, 89

Haggai

2:4–5 113

Malachi

4:2 40

Wisdom of Solomon

1:7 113
7:27 104

NEW TESTAMENT

Matthew

11:27 116
23:9–10 86
28:19 16, 81, 97–98, 110, 119

Mark

13:32 129

John

1:1 20, 72n14, 102
1:3 56, 82n8, 89
1:6 80
1:9 71, 76, 116, 116n20
1:12 87
1:14 124
3:6 41n42
3:8 105
4:7 129
4:14 101–2
4:24 18, 116
7:29 102n31
8:12 76
8:42 102n31
10:27–28 87
12:35 40
12:45 73
12:49 39
14:16 76, 84
14:26 80, 87, 103
14:28 20, 55, 72
15:26 103
16:7 103
16:13 39–40
16:15 102
17:3 54–55
17:8 102n31
17:10 102
20:17 55n16

Acts of the Apostles

2:36 56, 75
7:22 30n21

Romans

8:2 102n32
8:3 130
8:11 87
8:15 87
8:26–27 115n15
8:29 57, 57n21
12:6 112

1 Corinthians

1:20 32
1:24 33, 72n17, 102
1:30 72n17
2:4 76
2:6 32
2:11–12 87, 98
3:16 88n17
8:6 53, 53n12, 56
12:3 116–117
12:4–6 87
12:11 87–88, 103, 105
15:35–47 127

2 Corinthians

3 32n26, 115n17
4:4–6 32n26, 74

Galatians

4:4–6 80

Ephesians

1:18 32n26
2:21–22 88, 88n17

Philippians

2:6 76

Colossians

1:15 72n17, 74, 102

1 Timothy

5:21 118n23
6:13 87
6:16 71

Hebrews

1:3 66, 72, 72n17
1:14 80, 99, 105, 105n39
6:4 32n26
10:32 32n26

1 Peter

2:22 130

1 John

3:24 88n17